RANDOM
WEBSTER'S

HANDY

GRAMMAR, USAGE & PUNCTUATION

SECOND EDITION

RANDOM HOUSE REFERENCE
NEW YORK · TORONTO · LONDON · SYDNEY · AUCKLAND

Random House *Webster's Handy Grammar, Usage, and Punctuation,*
2nd edition

Copyright © 2001 by Random House, Inc.

All rights reserved under International and Pan-American Copyright
Conventions. No part of this book may be reproduced in any form or by
any means, electronic or mechanical, including photocopying, without the
written permission of the publisher. All inquiries should be addressed to
Random House Reference, Random House, Inc., 1745 Broadway, New
York, NY 10019. Published in the United States by Random House, Inc.,
New York and simultaneously in Canada by Random House of Canada
Limited.

This work was originally published in 2001 by Random House as
Random House Webster's Pocket Grammar, Usage, and Punctuation,
Second Edition.

Random House is a registered trademark of Random House, Inc.

This book is available for special purchases in bulk by organizations
and institutions, not for resale, at special discounts. Please direct your sales
inquiries to the Random House Premium Sales Department,
fax 212-572-4961.

Please address inquiries about electronic licensing of reference products,
for use on a network or in software or on CD-ROM, to the Subsidiary Rights
Department, Random House Reference, fax 212-940-7352.

Visit the Random House Web site at www.randomhouse.com.

Library of Congress Cataloging-in-Publication Data is available
upon request.

Printed in the United States of America.

0 9 8 7

June 2003

ISBN-13: 978-0-375-72005-5

CONTENTS

SECTION 1: GRAMMAR

PARTS OF SPEECH   3

NOUNS   4
PRONOUNS   6
Case   9
Ambiguous References   17
VERBS   19
Transitive Verbs   19
Intransitive Verbs   19
Ergative Verbs   20
Copula Verbs   20
Auxiliary Verbs   22
Phrasal Verbs   23
Verbal Forms   24
Regular and
   Irregular Verbs   26
Tense   30
Mood   40
Voice   42
Verbals   44
DETERMINERS   45
ADJECTIVES   46
Nouns and
   Pronouns as Adjectives   46
Special Adjectives   47
ADVERBS   48
Sentence Adverbs   49
ADJECTIVE OR ADVERB?   49
Using Adjectives
   after Linking Verbs   51

Using Adjectives or Adverbs
  after Direct Objects 52
Words That Can Be Either
  Adjectives or Adverbs 53
Using Adjectives and Adverbs
  to Make Comparisons 53

PREPOSITIONS   **58**
Common Prepositions 58
Phrasal Prepositions 59
Prepositional Phrases 59
Placement of Prepositions 60
Prepositional Phrases as
  Adverbs and Adjectives 60
Preposition or Adverb 61

CONJUNCTIONS   **61**
Coordinating Conjunctions 62
Correlative Conjunctions 63
Subordinating Conjunctions 64
Subordinating Conjunction
  or Preposition? 65
Conjunctive Adverb
  or Transitional Phrase? 66
Transitional Phrase 67
Transitional Phrase or Co-
  ordinating Conjunction? 68

INTERJECTIONS   **68**

PHRASES   **70**
Noun Phrases 70
Verb Phrases 70
Prepositional Phrases 70
Verbal Phrases 71

CLAUSES   **72**
Independent Clauses 72
Dependent Clauses 72

Adjective Clauses **73**
Adverb Clauses **73**
Noun Clauses **74**
Elliptical Clauses **75**

SENTENCES   76

SUBJECTS AND PREDICATES   76
HARD TO LOCATE SUBJECTS   76
Commands or Directions **76**
Questions **77**
Sentences Beginning
with *There* or *Here* **77**
Inverted Sentences **78**

SENTENCE COMPLEMENTS   78
Direct Objects **78**
Indirect Objects **79**
Object Complements **79**
Subject Complements **80**

FORMING SENTENCES   80
Simple Sentences **81**
Compound Sentences **81**
Complex Sentences **82**
Compound-Complex
Sentences **83**

REVIEW OF SENTENCE FORMS   83
SENTENCE FUNCTIONS   84
Declarative Sentences **84**
Interrogative Sentences **84**
Imperative Sentences **85**
Exclamatory Sentences **85**

SENTENCE ERRORS   86
Fragments **86**
Run-ons **88**
Misplaced Modifiers **90**
Dangling Modifiers **91**

Squinting Modifiers   93
AGREEMENT OF SENTENCE PARTS   **94**
Subject-Verb Agreement   95
Pronoun-Antecedent
Agreement   102

SHIFTS   **105**
SHIFTS IN TENSE   **105**
SHIFTS IN VOICE   **106**
SHIFTS IN MOOD   **107**
SHIFTS IN PERSON   **108**
SHIFTS IN PERSPECTIVE   **110**
SHIFTS IN NUMBER   **110**
Person and Number with
Collective Nouns   111
SHIFTS IN TONE AND STYLE   **112**
SHIFTS IN DIRECT AND
INDIRECT QUOTATIONS   **114**

PARALLELISM   **116**
PARALLEL STRUCTURE   **116**
PARALLEL ITEMS IN SERIES   **118**
PARALLEL OUTLINES AND LISTS   **119**

SECTION 2: USAGE

COMMON ERRORS   **123**

COMMONLY
CONFUSED WORDS   **167**

AVOIDING INSENSITIVE AND
OFFENSIVE LANGUAGE   **200**
SEXISM   **201**
Replacing *Man* or *Men*   202

Using Gender-Neutral
Terms for Occupations,
Positions, Roles, Etc.   **202**
Avoiding Generic Use of
the Personal Pronouns
He, *His*, and *Him*   **204**
Referring to Members of Both
Sexes with Parallel Names,
Titles, or Descriptions   **205**

RACE, ETHNICITY, AND
NATIONAL ORIGIN   206
AGE   207
SEXUAL ORIENTATION   208
AVOIDING DEPERSONALIZATION
OF PERSONS WITH DISABILITIES
OR ILLNESSES   208
AVOIDING PATRONIZING OR
DEMEANING EXPRESSIONS   209
AVOIDING LANGUAGE THAT
EXCLUDES OR UNNECESSARILY
EMPHASIZES DIFFERENCES   210

SECTION 3: SPELLING

SPELLING RULES   215

WORDS COMMONLY
MISSPELLED   218

USING A SPELL
CHECKER   231

RULES OF WORD
DIVISION   232

SECTION 4: PUNCTUATION

PERIOD   235
QUESTION MARK   236
EXCLAMATION POINT   237
COMMA   237
SEMICOLON   243
COLON   245
DASH   247
ELLIPSIS   249
PARENTHESES   250
BRACKETS   251
QUOTATION MARKS   253
ITALICS/UNDERLINING   255
FORWARD SLASH   257
APOSTROPHE   257
HYPHEN   260
CAPITALIZATION   263

SECTION 5: PREFIXES, SUFFIXES AND ROOTS

COMMON PREFIXES
    AND THEIR MEANINGS   269

COMMON SUFFIXES
    AND THEIR MEANINGS   276

COMMON ROOTS
    AND THEIR MEANINGS   287

INDEX

INDEX   303

Grammar

PARTS OF SPEECH

The English language has nine basic classes of words, or parts of speech: **nouns, pronouns, verbs, adjectives, determiners, adverbs, prepositions, conjunctions**, and **interjections**.

Words often serve more than one grammatical function, depending on their position, meaning, and use in a sentence. Therefore, the same word can be a different part of speech in different sentences. For example, the word *help* can be either a verb or a noun.

Help as a noun:

The offer of **help** was greatly appreciated.

(Here *help* is the name of something.)

Help as a verb:

They **help** the community by volunteering their time to tutor illiterate adults.

(Here *help* expresses an action.)

Since words can work in different ways, you must determine how the word is functioning within a sentence before you can label it as a specific part of speech. You cannot assume that any word will always be the same part of speech and fulfill the same grammatical function.

Words and phrases from different parts of speech often modify other words and phrases. For instance, an adjective modifies a noun by describing the noun (a **blue** hat). An adverb modifies an adjective, a verb, or another adverb by giving more specific information about it (a **light** blue hat; He spoke **quickly**; He spoke **very quickly**).

NOUNS

A *noun* is a word used to name a person, place, thing, idea, state, or quality.

Person	**Place**	**Thing**
Mary	library	flowers
Edward	Ontario	mutiny
American	coastline	computer
cousin	Paris	house
Mr. Jones	city	rabbit

Idea	**State**	**Quality**
democracy	hunger	integrity
equality	poverty	courage
Hinduism	happiness	sincerity
justice	rage	decency
evil	joy	bravery

Some of the nouns listed above can be further classified into specific types.

Common nouns name any of a class of people, places, or things:

girl
city
river
road

Proper nouns name specific people, places, and things:

    Lisa
    Vienna
    Ohio River
    Main Street

Collective nouns name groups of people or things:

    team
    clan
    flock
    tribe
    pack
    committee

Mass nouns name qualities or things that cannot be counted and do not have plural forms:

    laughter
    sand
    valor
    exhaustion
    anger
    wheat

Compound nouns are made up of two or more words. The words may be separate, hyphenated, or combined:

    boarding pass
    mother-in-law
    housework
    runaway
    airport
    schoolroom

Pronouns

A *pronoun* is a word that takes the place of a noun.

> Ellen has been working on the project for a long time. **She** spends eight hours a day on it. **Her** time is well spent, however, as **she herself** recognizes.

Antecedents

An *antecedent* is the noun, phrase, clause, or sentence to which a pronoun refers. Use a singular pronoun to refer to a singular antecedent and a plural pronoun to refer to a plural antecedent. In the above example, the antecedent of the pronoun *she* is *Ellen;* the antecedent of the pronoun *it* is *project.*

Types of Pronouns

Personal pronouns refer to the one speaking, the one spoken to, or the one spoken about. Personal pronouns that refer to the speaker are known as *first-person pronouns;* those that refer to the person spoken to are known as *second-person pronouns;* those that refer to the person, place, or thing spoken about are known as *third-person pronouns.*

Singular

First person	I	me	my, mine
Second person	you	you	your, yours
Third person	he	him	his
	she	her	her, hers
	it	it	its

Plural

First person	we	us	our, ours
Second person	you	you	your, yours
Third person	they	them	their, theirs

Intensive pronouns and reflexive pronouns end in *-self* or *-selves*.

myself	ourselves
yourself	yourselves
himself	themselves
herself	themselves
itself	

Intensive pronouns add emphasis to a noun or pronoun:

I **myself** have never given much thought to the matter.

Mary hung the striped wallpaper **herself**.

Reflexive pronouns show that the subject of the sentence also receives the action of the verb:

I treated **myself** to a new pair of shoes.

Michael kept telling **himself** that it was not his fault.

Interrogative pronouns are used to ask questions. These pronouns do not have to have a specific antecedent.

which   what   who   whom   whose

What did you call me for in the first place?

Whom have you called about this matter?

Whose is that?

Relative pronouns are used to tie together or relate groups of words. Relative pronouns begin subordinate clauses.

which   what   who   whom   whose

Debbie enrolled in the class **that** her employer recommended.

Charles has a friend **who** lives in Toronto.

Demonstrative pronouns are used to point out nouns, phrases, or clauses. They can be placed before or after their antecedents.

this   that   these   those

This is the book I told you about last week.

That is a perfect place to sit down and have lunch.

Is **that** the house with the Japanese garden in the back yard?

Indefinite pronouns take the place of a noun but do not have to have a specific antecedent. Following is a list of some common indefinite pronouns.

all	everything	none
another	few	nothing
any	little	one
anybody	many	other
anyone	more	others
anything	most	several
both	much	some
each	neither	somebody
either	no one	someone
everybody	nobody	something

Indefinite pronouns can have a specific antecedent or no specific antecedent.

Specific Antecedent

The **casserole** was so delicious that **none** was left by the end of the meal.

A **few** of the **relatives** usually lend a hand when my husband undertakes one of his home-repair projects.

No Specific Antecedent

Someone arrived at the party early, much to the embarrassment of the unprepared host and hostess.

Everyone stayed late, too.

CASE

The majority of English words rely on their position within a sentence (not their form) to show their function. The placement of a word determines whether it is a subject or object. Certain nouns and pronouns, however, also change their form to indicate their use.

Case is the form of a noun or pronoun that shows how it is used and how it relates to other words in a sentence.

English has three cases: **nominative**, **objective**, and **possessive**. In general, pronouns take the nominative case when they function as the subject of a sentence or clause and the objective case when they function as the object of a verb or a preposition. Pronouns and nouns take the possessive case to indicate ownership.

Nouns change form only in the possessive case: for example, a **dog's** bone, **Maria's** hair. Some pronouns, in contrast, change form in the nominative, objective, and possessive cases. The following table shows how personal pronouns change form in the three different cases.

Nominative	Objective	Possessive
I	me	my, mine
you	you	your, yours
he	him	his
she	her	her, hers
it	it	its
we	us	our, ours
you	you	your, yours
they	them	their, theirs

Nominative Case

The *nominative case* is sometimes called the *subjective case* because it is used when pronouns function as subjects. The following examples illustrate how personal pronouns are used in the nominative case.

Subject of a Verb

We understand that they will be late.

Neither **she** nor **I** will be attending.

Appositive Identifying a Subject

An *appositive* is a word or a phrase appearing next to a noun or pronoun that explains or identifies it and is equivalent to it:

Both physicists, **Marie Curie and he,** worked on isolating radium.

Mr. Brown, **our English teacher**, went on the class trip with us.

Predicate Nominative

The *predicate nominative* is the noun or pronoun after a linking verb that renames the subject. The linking verb *to be* functions as an equals sign: the words on either side must be in the same case.

It is **I**.
The primary supervisor is **she**.
The fastest runners are **Lenore** and **he**.

Since the predicate nominative can sound overly formal in speech, many people use the colloquial: It's **me**. It's **her**. In formal speech and edited writing, however, the nominative forms should be used: It must be **he**. The person at the door was **she**, not her husband. This is **she**. In some instances, revising the sentence can produce a less artificial sound.

Predicate nominative

The delegates who represented the community at last evening's town board meeting were **he** and **I**.

Revision

He and **I** were the delegates who represented the community at last evening's town board meeting.

Objective Case

The *objective case* is used when a personal pronoun is a direct object, indirect object, or object of a preposition.

Direct Object

Bob's jokes embarrassed **me**.

When you reach the station, call either **him** or **me**.

Indirect Object

The glaring sun gave **my friends** and **me** a headache.

My aunt brought **us** pottery from Mexico.

Please give **him** some money.

Object of a Preposition

The cat leaped onto the bed and curled up beside **me**.

They fully understood why she had come with **us** rather than with **him**.

Let's keep the understanding between **you** and **me**.

Case after Than or As

If the word following *than* or *as* begins a clause, the pronoun takes the nominative case. If the word following *than* or *as* does not begin a clause, the pronoun takes the objective case. In some instances, the case depends on the meaning of the sentence. To help decide whether the sentence requires a pronoun in the nominative or objective case, complete the clause.

She has been working at Smithson longer than **he** (has).

Kevin is more proficient at marketing than **I** (am).

They are going to be informed as quickly as **we** (are).

I have stayed with Julia as long as **she** (has stayed with her).

I have stayed with Julia as long as (I have stayed with) **her**.

Uses of Who and Whom

The form of the pronoun *who* depends on its function within a clause.

Subordinate Clauses and Who/Whom

In subordinate clauses, use *who* and *whoever* for all subjects, *whom* and *whomever* for all objects, regardless of whether the clause itself acts as a subject or object:

Distribute the food to **whoever** needs it.

(Since *whoever* is the subject of *needs*, it is in the nominative case. The entire clause *whoever needs it* is the object of the preposition *to*.)

We did not realize **whom** the specialist had called.

(Since *whom* is the object of *called*, it is in the objective case. The entire clause *whom the specialist had called* is the object of the verb *realize*.)

Frederick is the lawyer **whom** most people hire for this type of work.

(Since *whom* is the object of *hire*, it is in the objective case. The clause *whom most people hire for this type of work* modifies the noun *lawyer*.)

> She is the candidate **who** everyone thinks will win.

(Since *who* is the subject of *will win*, it is in the nominative case. The clause *who everyone thinks will win* modifies the noun *candidate*.)

> There is only one doctor **who** I know makes house calls.

(Since *who* is the subject of *makes*, it is in the nominative case. The clause *who makes house calls* modifies the noun *doctor*.)

> He will speak to **whoever** will listen.

(Since *whoever* is the subject of *will listen*, it is in the nominative case. The clause *whoever will listen* is the object of the preposition *to*.)

Questions and Who/Whom

Use *who* at the beginning of a question about a subject; use *whom* at the beginning of a question about an object.

In informal speech, the distinction is not always made, and *who* is used for the first word of a question, regardless of whether the question is about a subject or an object.

To determine whether to use *who* or *whom*, you can use a personal pronoun to construct an answer to the question. The case of the personal pronoun determines whether *who* (nominative) or *whom* (objective) is required:

Who left the car doors open?

(Possible answer to the question: "He left the car doors open." Since *he* is in the nominative case, the question is about a subject and thus requires *who*.)

Whom should I see about this invoice?

(Possible answer to the question: "You should see him." Since *him* is in the objective case, the question is about an object and thus requires *whom*.)

Possessive Case

Use the *possessive case* of a pronoun to show ownership.

The possessives *my, mine; your, yours; her, hers; our, ours;* and *their, theirs* have two different forms. Which one you use depends on whether the possessive comes before a noun or takes the place of a noun. *His* and *its* are used in either position.

Use the possessive pronouns *my, her, your, our, their* before a noun:

My cat sleeps all day.

Where is **your** umbrella?

Joan left **her** coat in the theater.

Our son is graduating from high school this year.

Use the possessive pronouns *mine, hers, yours, ours, theirs* alone to indicate possession:

This idea was **mine**, not **yours**.

Is this article really **hers**?

Do you believe that it's **theirs**?

The red one is **ours**.

In most instances you should use the possessive case before gerunds.

A *gerund* is the *-ing* form of the verb (*swimming, snoring*) used as a noun. Possessive pronouns and nouns often precede gerunds, as in:

The landlord objected to **my** (not *me*) having guests late at night.

My shoveling the snow saved the mail carrier a nasty fall.

Do you mind **my** eating the rest of the cake?

She wholeheartedly supported **his** exercising.

My colleagues were annoyed by **my** coughing.

A possessive is not used before a gerund if its use would create a clumsy sentence. In these instances, you should rewrite the sentence entirely to eliminate the awkward construction.

Awkward

The neighbors spread the news about **somebody's** wanting to organize a block party.

Revision

We heard from the neighbors that somebody wants to organize a block party.

Note: Never use an apostrophe with a possessive pronoun. The following personal pronouns are already possessive and have no need for an apostrophe: *my*, *mine*, *your*, *yours*, *her*, *hers*, *its*, *our*, *ours*, *their*, and *theirs*. Do not confuse the contraction *it's* (for *it is*) with the possessive pronoun *its*.

AMBIGUOUS REFERENCES

Make sure that the reference is clear when two pronouns could logically refer to either of two antecedents. The following examples demonstrate how ambiguities can occur.

Unclear

The manager told Mrs. Greenberger that **she** will have to train her new people by June.

As the sentence is written, it is unclear whether the manager or Mrs. Greenberger will have to train the new people and whose new people have to be trained.

Clearer

Since Mrs. Greenberger will have to train her new people by June, she decided to take her vacation in the fall.

If the reference to an antecedent is not specific, confusion can arise. An unclear pronoun reference can usually be clarified by rearranging the sentence or by using the noun rather than the pronoun, as the following examples show.

Unclear

When you have finished with the stamp and bound the report, please return **it** to the storeroom.

Clearer

When you have finished with the stamp and bound the report, please return the stamp to the storeroom.

Sometimes, using *it, they,* and *you* incorrectly will result in a sentence that is vague or wordy. Removing the pronoun, eliminating excess words, or revising the sentence helps produce a clearer and more vigorous style.

Wordy

In the cookbook **it** says that wooden chopping blocks should be disinfected with bleach.

Better

The cookbook says that wooden chopping blocks should be disinfected with bleach.

Wordy

They say you should use a cold steam vaporizer instead of the traditional hot steam one.

Better

The doctor recommends using a cold steam vaporizer instead of the traditional hot steam one.

VERBS

A *verb* is a word that expresses an action, an occurrence, or a state of being.

Action	Occurrence	State of Being
jump	become	be
swim	happen	seem
throw		
speak		

Action verbs can describe mental actions as well as physical actions. The verb *think*, for example, describes a mental action, one that cannot be seen. Additional examples of action verbs that describe unseen mental actions include *understand, welcome, enjoy, relish, ponder, consider*, and *deliberate*. Action verbs are divided into two groups, **transitive** and **intransitive**, depending on how they function within a sentence.

TRANSITIVE VERBS

A *transitive verb* is a verb that requires a direct object to complete its meaning. The direct object receives the action of the verb:

My son **ate** the last piece of chocolate cake.

My sister **baked** another cake.

Please **call** your mother.

Sally **read** twenty-five books during the summer.

INTRANSITIVE VERBS

An *intransitive verb* is a verb that does not need a direct object to complete its meaning:

When they heard about it, my friends **laughed**.

Even the baby **giggled**.

Please **sit** down.

I **worked** hard all winter.

ERGATIVE VERBS

Some verbs can treat the same noun as both a subject and an object. An *ergative* is a verb that allows the subject of the intransitive form to be the object of the transitive form:

The boat **capsized**.

They **capsized** the boat.

The dress **buttons** down the front.

She **buttoned** her dress.

Marie **sat**.

He **sat** the baby in her highchair.

The boat **sank** to the bottom of the lake.

They deliberately **sank** the boat.

The doorbell **rang**.

They **rang** the doorbell.

COPULA VERBS

A *copula*, or *linking verb*, describes an occurrence or a state of being. It connects parts of a sentence.

The most common linking verb is the verb *to be*. Following are some other linking verbs.

appear	seem
become	smell
feel	sound
grow	stay
look	taste
remain	

The supports **looked** fragile.

The actor **seemed** nervous when the play began.

It **sounds** like a fire alarm.

I **became** increasingly certain that he was lying.

The verbs on the list do not always function as linking verbs. To determine whether the word is functioning as a linking verb or as an action verb, examine its role in the sentence.

Linking verb

The child **grew** tired by the end of the evening.

The milk **smells** sour.

The lemonade **tastes** too sweet.

Action verb

My mother **grows** the best tomatoes I have ever eaten.

Can you **smell** those roses?

Have you **tasted** the lemonade?

A *subject complement* (noun, pronoun, or adjective) follows a linking verb and describes or identifies the subject.

My sister is **a pediatrician**.

The lemonade tastes **sour**.

Is that **you**?

I feel **sick**.

A subject complement is frequently a subject nominative. Since the linking verb serves as an equals sign, the words on both sides of it must be in the same case, i.e., the nominative case.

We all assumed that it was **he**.

I am waiting for my mother to call. Is that **she**?

AUXILIARY VERBS

An *auxiliary verb*, or *helping verb*, is used with a main verb to form a verb phrase. The three helping verbs are *be*, *do*, and *have*.

Are you **enjoying** the play?

Did you **complete** the project on time?

Have you ever **eaten** at the Chinese restaurant on 12th Street?

Modal Verbs

There is another class of auxiliary verbs called *modals*. These verbs express ability, possibility, obligation, permission, intention, and probability. The modal auxiliaries are *can*, *could*, *may*, *might*, *shall*, *should*, *will*, *would*, and *must*. *Dare*, *had better*, *have to*, *need*, *ought to*, and *used to* are also used as modals.

I **might work** late tonight.

Can you **help** me?

Could you please **help** me?

You really **should** not **do** that.

May I please **have** a cup of coffee?

I **must go** to the office early tomorrow morning.

You **had better do** your homework before you go out.

You **ought to try** it.

PHRASAL VERBS

A *phrasal verb* is a combination of a verb and one or more adverbs or prepositions. The meaning of the phrase is often idiomatic and is not predictable from the individual parts. Examples of phrasal verbs are: *call off, catch on, get along with, put up with, send for, show up, stand up to, take off, throw away*.

It won't take you long to **catch on** to the new routine.

She has trouble **getting along with** her coworkers.

What time did they finally **show up**?

You ought to **stand up** to him.

Did your flight **take off** on time?

She has **thrown away** several opportunities.

VERBAL FORMS

All English verbs have four basic *forms*, or principal parts: the **infinitive**, the **past**, the **past participle**, and the **present participle**.

Infinitive Form

The *infinitive* is the basic form of a verb:

- to grin
- to talk
- to snore
- to walk
- to drop

The *bare infinitive* is the form found in dictionaries, without *to*:

- grin
- talk
- snore
- walk
- drop

The infinitive (*to* + the bare form of a verb) can begin a clause that acts as an object. Main verbs that invite infinitives as objects include *ask, beg, expect, help, intend, like, mean, prefer, want, wish, would hate,* and *would like*:

> We would like **to go** to Paris in June.

> They had not expected **to go** to Italy last winter.

> I would have liked **to hear** at least one of Mozart's operas during my trip to Vienna last year.

> She wanted **to win** that award.

Perfect Infinitive Form

The *perfect infinitive* (*to have* + the past participle) is used with a main verb in the present tense to express action that will be completed by a future date:

> They expect **to have seen** three plays by the time they return.

> We hope **to have moved** into our new house by Christmas.

The perfect infinitive is also used with *would like/love* to express a wish that was not realized:

> She would like **to have won** that award.

> He would love **to have bought** a new car.

Past Form

The *past* form is used to form the past tense. It indicates that the verb's action took place in the past. The past form of regular verbs is formed by adding *-d* or *-ed* to the infinitive, sometimes requiring the doubling of a final consonant. (See pp. 27–30 for irregular verbs.)

> grinned
> talked
> snored
> walked
> dropped

Past Participle

The *past participle* is used with at least one helping verb and/or modal verb to form the *perfect tenses*. The past participle of regular verbs is the same as the past form. (See pp. 27-30 for irregular verbs.)

grinned
talked
snored
walked
dropped

The past participle can also be used as an adjective:

Where is the **finished** product?

My nephew refuses to eat **cooked** vegetables.

Present Participle

The *present participle* is used with the verb *to be* to create *progressive forms*, which show continuing action. The present participle is formed by adding -*ing* to the infinitive. The final consonant is often doubled with this addition.

grinning
talking
snoring
walking
dropping

Like the past participle, the present participle can be used as an adjective:

Stand clear of the **closing** doors.

She picked up the **crying** child.

REGULAR AND IRREGULAR VERBS

The majority of English verbs are regular and change their form by adding -*ing*, -*ed*, or -*d* to the infinitive. However, many verbs do not follow this pattern. These irregular verbs form their past tense and past participle in a number of ways: some change an internal vowel and add -*n* to the past participle; some retain the same spelling in all three forms or in the past tense and past participle; some follow no discernible pattern.

The following list includes the most common irregular verbs. For information about verbs not included below, consult a dictionary. If a verb is regular, the dictionary will usually give only the infinitive. If the verb is irregular, the dictionary will include the past tense and past participle along with the infinitive; if only two forms are given, the past tense and the past participle are identical.

Common Irregular Verbs

Present Tense	Past Tense	Past Participle
arise	arose	arisen
be	was/were	been
bear	bore	borne, born
beat	beat	beaten
become	became	become
begin	began	begun
bend	bent	bent
bet	bet, betted	bet
bid	bid, bade	bid, bidden
bind	bound	bound
bite	bit	bitten
blow	blew	blown
break	broke	broken
bring	brought	brought

burn	burned, burnt	burned, burnt
burst	burst	burst
buy	bought	bought
catch	caught	caught
choose	chose	chosen
cling	clung	clung
come	came	come
creep	crept	crept
cut	cut	cut
deal	dealt	dealt
dig	dug	dug
dive	dived, dove	dived
do	did	done
draw	drew	drawn
dream	dreamed, dreamt	dreamed, dreamt
drink	drank	drunk
drive	drove	driven
eat	ate	eaten
fall	fell	fallen
fight	fought	fought
find	found	found
flee	fled	fled
fling	flung	flung
fly	flew	flown
forbid	forbade, forbad	forbidden, forbid
forget	forgot	forgotten, forgot
forgive	forgave	forgiven
freeze	froze	frozen
get	got	got, gotten
give	gave	given
go	went	gone

grow	grew	grown
hang (suspend)	hung	hung
hang (execute)	hanged	hanged
hear	heard	heard
hide	hid	hidden
hold	held	held
keep	kept	kept
kneel	knelt	knelt
know	knew	known
lay (put down)	laid	laid
lead	led	led
lie (rest; recline)	lay	lain
lose	lost	lost
mistake	mistook	mistaken
pay	paid	paid
ride	rode	ridden
ring	rang	rung
rise	rose	risen
run	ran	run
see	saw	seen
set	set	set
sew	sewed	sewed, sewn
shake	shook	shaken
shrink	shrank	shrunk
sing	sang, sung	sung
sit	sat	sat
slay	slew	slain
speak	spoke	spoken
spend	spent	spent
spring	sprang	sprung
stand	stood	stood
steal	stole	stolen
strike	struck	struck
swear	swore	sworn

sweep	swept	swept
swim	swam	swum
take	took	taken
teach	taught	taught
tear	tore	torn
throw	threw	thrown
wake	woke,	woken,
	waked	waked
wear	wore	worn
weep	wept	wept
win	won	won
wind	wound	wound
wring	wrung	wrung
write	wrote	written

TENSE

Tense refers to the form of a verb that indicates the time of the action, occurrence, or state of being expressed by the verb. Tense is different from time. The present tense, for instance, shows present time, but it can also indicate future time or a generally accepted belief.

English has two groups of tenses: the **simple tenses** (present, past, and future) and the **perfect tenses** (present perfect, past perfect, and future perfect).

Simple Tenses

The *simple tenses* generally show that an action or state of being is taking place now, in the future, or in the past relative to the speaker or writer. The simple tenses indicate a finished, momentary, or habitual action or condition.

Present:	smile (smiles)	go (goes)
Past:	smiled	went
Future:	will (shall) smile	will (shall) go

Note: Shall is rarely used except in formal speaking and writing, to express determination, and in laws or directives.

I **shall** call the governor myself.

We **shall** overcome.

You **shall** not go!

All new students **shall** report to the dean upon arrival.

Present Tense

Except when the subjects are singular nouns or third-person singular pronouns, the present tense is the same as the infinitive form of the verb (I walk – to walk, you skip – to skip, we jump – to jump, they catch – to catch). With singular nouns or third-person singular pronouns, -s or -es is added to the infinitive (Robert **walks**, she **skips**, he **jumps**, it **catches**).

The *present tense* is used:

To state present action

Nick **prepares** the walls for painting.

To show present condition

The secretary **is** efficient.

To show that an action occurs regularly

Louise **prepares** a report for her supervisor every week.

To show a condition that occurs regularly

> The traffic **is** usually backed up at the bridge in the evening.

To indicate future time, as an alternative to the future tense when a specific time is indicated

> The income tax refund **arrives** tomorrow.

To state a generally held belief

> Haste **makes** waste.

To state a scientific truth

> A body in motion **tends** to stay in motion.

To discuss literary works, films, etc.

> In *Hamlet*, Claudius **poisons** his brother, **marries** his former sister-in-law, and **seizes** the throne.

To narrate historical events as if they were happening in the present time (the "historical present")

> In 1781 Cornwallis **surrenders** to Washington at Yorktown.

Past Tense

The *past tense* of regular verbs is formed by adding -*d* or -*ed* to the infinitive. The past tense of irregular verbs is formed in a variety of ways. Consult the table on pages 27-30 for forms of irregular verbs.

The *past tense* is used:

To show actions and conditions that began and ended in the past, or were true at a particular time in the past

Johnny **walked** the dog last night.

Joan **was** very happy.

To show recurring past actions that do not extend to the present

During World War II, Eric **saw** the fighting through the lens of a camera.

Future Tense

The *future tense* is formed by using the modal verbs *will* or *shall* plus the bare infinitive form of the verb.

The *future tense* is used:

To show a future action

Tomorrow the sun **will set** at 6:45 P.M.

To show a future condition

They **will be** excited when they see the presents.

To indicate intention

The Board of Education has announced that it **will begin** repairs on the pool as soon as possible.

To show probability

The decrease in land values in the Northeast **will** most likely **continue** into next year.

Perfect Tenses

The *perfect tenses* indicate that one action was or will be finished before an indicated time.

Present:	have (has) smiled	have (has) gone
Past:	had smiled	had gone
Future:	will (shall) have smiled	will (shall) have gone

Present Perfect

The *present perfect* tense is formed by using the present tense of the auxiliary verb *have* plus the past participle of the main verb.

The *present perfect* tense is used:

To show completed action

Martin **has finished** talking to his clients.

To show past action or condition continuing into the present

We **have been** waiting for a week.

To show action that occurred at an unspecified past time

I **have reviewed** all the new procedures.

Past Perfect

The *past perfect* tense is formed by using the past tense of the auxiliary verb *have* plus the past participle of the main verb.

The *past perfect* tense is used:

To show one action or condition completed before another

> By the time her employer returned, Linda **had completed** all her assigned tasks.

To show an action that occurred before a specific past time

> By 1930 insulin **had been** isolated, refined, and distributed.

To show that something that was assumed or expected did not in fact happen

> We **had hoped** to have the new cabin ready by the first of June.

Future Perfect

The *future perfect* tense is formed by using the auxiliary verbs *will* and *have* plus the past participle of the main verb.

The *future perfect* tense is used:

To show a future action or condition completed before another

> By the time you read this letter, Bill **will have left** California for Mexico.

To show that an action will be completed by a specific future time

> By tomorrow the bonds **will have lost** over fifty percent of their face value.

Progressive Forms

Progressive forms are verb phrases that show continuing action. They are created by using the present participle of the main verb with forms of the verbs *to be* and *to have*.

Present Progressive

The *present progressive* is used to show continuing action or condition. It is formed with the present form of the verb *to be* plus the present participle:

> I **am finishing** the painting while the children are at camp.

> Medicine **is becoming** increasingly specialized.

Past Progressive

The *past progressive* is used to show an action or condition continuing in the past and to show two past actions occurring simultaneously. It is formed with the past form of the verb *to be* plus the present participle:

> She **was becoming** disenchanted with the protein diet.

> Garth fell off his bike while he **was watching** a cat climb a tree.

Future Progressive

The *future progressive* is used to show continuing future action and to show continuing action at a specific future time. It is formed with *will* plus *be* plus the present participle:

> She **will be studying** all night.

Will you **be traveling** to Japan again in the spring?

Present Perfect Progressive

The *present perfect progressive* is used to show that an action or condition is continuing from the past into the present and/or the future. It is formed with the present form of the verb *to have* plus *been* plus the present participle:

The amount of pollution **has been increasing** sharply.

I **have been waiting** for a train for fifteen minutes.

Past Perfect Progressive

The *past perfect progressive* is used to show that a continuing past action has been interrupted by another. It is formed with *had* plus *been* plus the present participle:

Alice **had been taking** a detour through town until the new bridge was finished.

The workers **had been planning** a strike when the management made a new offer.

Future Perfect Progressive

The *future perfect progressive* is used to show that an action or condition will continue until a specific time in the future. It is formed with *will* plus *have* plus *been* plus the present participle:

By Monday I **will have been working** on that project for a month.

In September they **will have been traveling** for nearly a year.

Using Tenses

The *sequence of tenses* refers to the relationship among the verbs within a sentence or in sentences that follow each other. Illogical shifts in verb tenses confuse readers and muddle meaning. For clarity and sense, all the verbs must accurately reflect changes in time in the real world. Using tenses correctly allows you to express the desired sequence of events correctly.

Simultaneous Actions

If the actions described occur at approximately the same time, the tenses of all the verbs must be the same.

The audience **applauded** when the conductor **mounted** the podium.

Although we **have analyzed** the data, we **have** not **been able** to come to a firm conclusion.

William Carlos Williams **was** a pediatrician in Paterson, New Jersey, who **wrote** some of the most distinctive verse of the twentieth century.

Actions Occurring at Different Times

If the verbs within a sentence describe actions that have occurred, are occurring, or will occur at different times, the tenses of the verbs must be different to express the different time sequence.

The conference **had been over** for an hour by the time I **arrived**.

I **asked** if he **had consulted** his attorney last week.

Joe **was** worried that his dog **had bitten** the mail carrier.

Conditional Sentences

When the realization of the situation described in the main clause depends on something else, a *conditional clause* is used. Conditional clauses usually begin with *if* or *unless*.

We'll stay home **if** it rains.

We'll go **unless** it rains.

If the situation described is likely to occur, use the present tense in the conditional clause and *will* (or *won't*) in the main clause:

If you **take** the train, you **will be** in the center of the city by 3:00.

If you **wear** boots, your feet **won't get** cold.

If the situation described is imaginary or unlikely to occur, use the past tense form in the conditional clause and *would*, *might*, or *could* in the main clause.

If I **had** her address, I **could send** her flowers.

If wishes **were** horses, beggars **would ride**.

If he **called** me, I **might go**.

If you want to describe a conditional situation that occurred in the past, use the past perfect form in the conditional clause and *would have* in the main clause.

> If they **had arrived** on time, we **would have been** able to go to a movie.

> The curtains **would** not **have gotten** wet if I **had remembered** to close the windows.

Using Participles Logically

The present participle expresses action occurring at the same time as that of the main verb.

> **Chewing** his pencil absently, Jeremy stared out the window at the mountains in the distance.

The present perfect participle expresses action occurring before that of the main verb.

> **Having operated** the terminal for a month, the assistant knew how to repair the malfunction.

MOOD

The *mood* of a verb shows how the writer or speaker regards what he or she is saying. The form of the verb changes to indicate the mood. In English, there are three moods: the **indicative**, the **imperative**, and the **subjunctive**.

Indicative Mood

The *indicative* mood is used to state a fact or to ask a question:

> Henry James **wrote** *The Turn of the Screw*.

> We **hold** soccer games only on Saturdays.

Did T. S. Eliot **have** a great impact on twentieth-century literature?

Do you **hold** soccer games only on Saturdays?

Imperative Mood

The *imperative* mood is used to give directions or express commands. Frequently, the subject (usually *you*) is understood rather than stated. *Let's* or *let us* can be used before the basic form of the verb in a command:

Get up!

Let's go to Mario's for dinner.

Turn left at the convenience store.

Subjunctive Mood

The *subjunctive* mood has traditionally been used to state wishes or desires, requirements, suggestions, or conditions that are contrary to fact. Its form looks different only in the present and past tenses of the verb *to be* and in the third-person singular present tense of all other verbs.

Although it has largely disappeared from English, the subjunctive survives in sentences with conditional clauses that are contrary to fact and in subordinate clauses after verbs like *wish*. In these cases, the subjunctive requires the form *were*:

He acted as if he **were** the owner.

If I **were** you, I would write them a letter.

I wish I **were** more organized.

The subjunctive is required in clauses expressing resolution, demand, or recommendation. In these cases, the subjunctive requires the bare infinitive form of the verb:

I move that the minutes **be** accepted.

He recommended that she **hire** an attorney.

They demanded that he **come** immediately.

The subjunctive is also used in certain idioms and set phrases:

Far **be** it from me . . .

If need **be** . . .

Be that as it may.

The people **be** damned.

Come rain or **come** shine.

As it **were** . . .

Suffice it to say . . .

Come what may . . .

VOICE

Voice shows whether the subject of a verb acts or is acted upon. There are two voices, **active** and **passive**. Only transitive verbs (those that take objects) can show voice.

Active Voice

When the subject of the verb does the action, the verb is in the *active voice:*

I **hit** the ball across the field.

The subject, *I*, does the action, *hit*.

Passive Voice

When the subject of the verb receives the action, the verb is in the *passive voice:*

The ball **was hit** by me.

The subject, *the ball*, receives the action, *was hit*.

To convert an active verb to a passive verb, a form of *to be* is used with the past participle.

Active

The storms **damaged** many homes.

Mary's dog **bit** Christopher.

Keats **wrote** "The Eve of St. Agnes."

Eileen **will make** dinner.

Passive

Many homes **were damaged** by the storms.

Christopher **was bitten** by Mary's dog.

"The Eve of St. Agnes" **was written** by Keats.

Dinner **will be made** by Eileen.

When to Use the Active Voice

In general, use the active voice to emphasize the performer of the action. Except for a small number of specific situations, which are described below, the active voice is usually clearer and more powerful than the passive voice.

When to Use the Passive Voice

The passive voice is preferable to the active voice:

> When you do not wish to mention the performer of the action
>
>> A mistake **has been made**.
>>
>> A check **has been returned** marked "insufficient funds."
>
> When it is necessary to avoid vagueness
>
>> Furniture **is manufactured** in Hickory, North Carolina.
>
> (Recasting this sentence in the active voice—"They manufacture furniture in Hickory, North Carolina"—results in the vague *they*.)
>
> When the performer of the action is not known
>
>> Plans for fifty units of low-income housing **were unveiled** at today's county meeting.
>>
>> The computer **was stolen**.
>
> When the result of the action is more important than the person performing the action
>
>> The driver **was arrested** for speeding.
>>
>> The chief suspect **was freed** on bail pending trial.

VERBALS

A *verbal* is a verb form—a *participle*, a *gerund*, or an *infinitive*—used as another part of speech. Verbals can function as nouns, adjectives, or adverbs.

Verbals can be modified by adverbs and adverbial phrases. They can also take objects and complements, but they cannot function as the only verb form in a sentence. The verbal phrase includes the verbal and the words related to it.

Signs **hung on this wall** will be removed.

(*Hung on this wall* is a participial phrase functioning as an adjective and modifying *signs*.)

Eating a low-fat diet reduces the risk of many diseases.

(*Eating a low-fat diet* is a gerund phrase functioning as a noun. It is the subject of the verb *reduces*.)

She likes **to read science fiction novels**.

(*To read science fiction novels* is an infinitive phrase functioning as a noun. It is the object of the verb *likes*.)

DETERMINERS

A *determiner*, sometimes also called a *noun marker*, is a word that determines the use of a noun without actually modifying it. Determiners are placed before nouns or noun phrases.

Examples of determiners are the articles *a*, *an*, and *the*; the demonstrative pronouns *this*, *that*, *these*, and *those*; the possessive pronouns *my*, *your*, *her*, *his*, *our*, *their*; and indefinite pronouns such as *some* and *each*.

ADJECTIVES

An *adjective* is a word that modifies (describes) a noun or a pronoun.

> The illness has affected **twelve** people in the apartment complex.

> We could give you **additional** reasons why that would not be a **wise** decision, but we believe these will suffice.

> You have had **enough** cookies for one day.

> The **gold** earrings go with that outfit much better than the **silver** ones do.

> The **eerie** noise seems to come from the basement.

> This is the **third** time I've asked you to clean your room!

> The **red**, **white**, and **blue** eye shadow proclaimed her patriotism but did little for her appearance.

NOUNS AND PRONOUNS AS ADJECTIVES

Nouns and pronouns can also function as adjectives.

> The **produce** stand is open all night.

> He has always enjoyed **piano** concertos.

> We look forward to our **coffee** break.

Some common phrases in which nouns are used as adjectives:

amusement park	**flood** control
apple pie	**flower** bed
art history	**horse** trailer
beach towel	**Star** Wars
child care	**truth** serum
dance class	**water** cooler

The demonstrative pronouns *this, that, these, those*; the interrogative pronouns *which* and *what*; and the indefinite pronouns *some, another, both, few, many, most, more*, etc., can all function as adjectives as well.

Are **those** socks yours or his?

This bus is rarely on time in the winter.

Which chores do you dislike the least?

What hobbies and sports do you enjoy the most?

Some people have managed to get tickets for the concert.

Any fan who wanted tickets had to be at the stadium at 4:00 A.M.

SPECIAL ADJECTIVES

There are also two special kinds of adjectives: *proper adjectives* and *compound adjectives*.

An adjective derived from a proper noun is called a *proper adjective*. Many of these adjectives are forms of people's names, as in *Emersonian*, from the nineteenth-century writer Ralph Waldo Emerson.

Kafkaesque situation
Shavian wit (Shaw)
Italian food
Chinese silk
March madness

An adjective made up of two or more words is called a *compound adjective*. The words in a compound adjective may be combined or hyphenated.

nearsighted
soft-shelled
open-and-shut
hardworking
close-by

Note: A compound that is not hyphenated when it is another part of speech becomes hyphenated when it acts as an adjective placed before a noun.

Compare:

Is there a grocery store **close by**?

a **close-by** grocery store

ADVERBS

An *adverb* is a word that modifies (describes) a verb, an adjective, or another adverb.

Adverbs add description and detail to writing by more closely focusing the meaning of a verb, an adjective, or another adverb. They can sometimes provide a wider range of description than adjectives alone. They describe by telling *where*, *when*, *how*, or *to what extent*.

The pot boiled **over**.

The rain came **down**.

Yesterday it snowed; **today** it all melted.

The children **often** talk about going to Disneyland.

I **quickly** changed the topic.

The days are **slowly** getting longer.

Wash your hands **thoroughly**, please.

The child has **fully** recovered from her illness.

SENTENCE ADVERBS

Sentence adverbs are adverbs that modify or comment on the sentence as a whole or on the conditions under which the sentence is spoken.

Frankly, I don't believe him.

Really, you are too clever for me.

Compare:

"Things will be all right," she said **hopefully**.

(The adverb *hopefully* modifies *said*.)

"**Hopefully**, things will be all right," she said.

(The sentence adverb *hopefully* modifies the full statement.)

ADJECTIVE OR ADVERB?

How can you tell if a word is an adjective or an adverb? Many adverbs end in *-ly*, but this is not a reliable way to distinguish adverbs from adjectives. Not all adverbs end in *-ly* (*far, fast, little, well*). There are some adjectives that end in *-ly* (*curly, surly, lovely*) and some adverbs that have two different forms. The best test for determining whether a word is an adjective or an adverb is to determine its purpose in the sentence. Adjectives modify nouns. Adverbs modify adjectives, verbs, and other adverbs. Ultimately, the part of speech is determined by a word's function in the sentence, not by its ending.

Examples of adverbs that have two forms:

He aims **high** in his political ambitions.

I don't care for **highly** seasoned food.

Look **sharp**!

The car swerved **sharply** to the left.

Don't arrive too **late**.

He has been sick a lot **lately**.

Don't talk so **loud**.

"I want to go home," my daughter said **loudly**.

Winter is drawing **near**.

He **nearly** fell into the ditch.

You did it **wrong** again.

You were blamed **wrongly**.

In some instances, the choice of form depends on the idiomatic use of the word. *Nearly*, for example, is used to mean *almost*, while *near* is used to mean *close in time*. *Slow* is used in spoken commands with short verbs that express motion, such as *drive* and *run* (Drive slow), and combined with present participles to form adjectives (a slow-moving vehicle). *Slowly* is commonly found in writing and is used in both speech and writing before a verb (He slowly swam across the cove) as well as after a verb (He swam slowly through the waves).

In general, the short forms are used more often in informal speech and writing; the long forms are found more often in formal discourse.

USING ADJECTIVES AFTER LINKING VERBS

A *linking verb* connects a subject with its complement (a **noun**, **pronoun**, or **adjective** that completes the meaning of the verb). Do not use an adverb after a linking verb.

The words that follow linking verbs are called *subject complements*. The most common linking verbs include forms of *to be*; verbs such as *appear, seem, believe, become, grow, turn, prove,* and *remain*; and sensory verbs such as *sound, look, hear, smell, feel,* and *taste.*

The dog **smelled** bad.

The girl **appeared** content.

The cold milk **tasted** good.

That **sounds** wonderful.

She **grew** thoughtful.

USING ADJECTIVES OR ADVERBS AFTER DIRECT OBJECTS

If the verb's direct object is followed by a word that describes the verb, that word must be an adverb.

He muttered the words **angrily**.

(The adverb *angrily* modifies the verb *muttered*.)

On the other hand, if the direct object is followed by a word that describes the object, the word must be an adjective.

The red pepper made the soup **spicy**.

(The adjective *spicy* modifies the noun *soup*.)

Compare the following pairs of sentences:

His mother called him **quiet**.

(The adjective *quiet* modifies the pronoun *him*.)

His mother called him **quietly**.

(The adverb *quietly* modifies the verb *called*.)

The evaluation committee considered the firm's work **complete**.

(The adjective *complete* modifies the noun *work*.)

The evaluation committee considered the firm's work **completely**.

(The adverb *completely* modifies the verb *considered*.)

WORDS THAT CAN BE EITHER ADJECTIVES OR ADVERBS

Depending on how they are used, some words can function as either adjectives or adverbs.

Adverb

I think you ought to go to bed **early** tonight.

Janine is fortunate that she lives **close** to public transportation.

Adjective

I had an **early** appointment this morning.

That certainly was a **close** call!

USING ADJECTIVES AND ADVERBS TO MAKE COMPARISONS

Many adjectives and adverbs take different forms when they are used to make comparisons. The three forms are the **positive degree**, the **comparative degree**, and the **superlative degree**.

Positive Degree

The *positive* degree is the basic form of the adjective or the adverb, the form listed in the dictionary. Since the positive degree does not indicate any comparison, the adjective or adverb does not change form.

Comparative Degree

The *comparative* form indicates a greater degree by comparing two things. In the comparative form, adjectives and adverbs add *-er* or *more*.

Superlative Degree

The *superlative* form indicates the greatest degree of difference or similarity by comparing three or more things. In this form, adjectives and adverbs add *-est* or *most*.

Choosing between Less/Least/ More/Most *and* -er/-est

A number of one- or two-syllable adjectives and adverbs use *-er* to form the comparative degree and *-est* to form the superlative degree. In some instances, these words use *more* and *most* when necessary to avoid awkwardness:

Positive	Comparative	Superlative
clear	clearer	clearest
poor	poorer	poorest
rich	richer	richest
pretty	prettier	prettiest
heavy	heavier	heaviest
steady	steadier	steadiest
childlike	more childlike	most childlike
youthful	more youthful	most youthful
golden	more golden	most golden

Most adjectives and adverbs of three or more syllables and nearly all adverbs ending in *-ly* use *more/less* and *most/least* to form the comparative and superlative degrees:

Positive	Comparative	Superlative
customary	more/ less customary	most/ least customary
regular	more/ less regular	most/ least regular
admiring	more/ less admiring	most/ least admiring
slowly	more/ less slowly	most/ least slowly
harshly	more/ less harshly	most/ least harshly
rudely	more/ less rudely	most/ least rudely

Irregular Adjectives and Adverbs

Some adverbs and adjectives are irregular in the comparative and superlative degrees, as shown in the table below:

Adjectives

Positive	Comparative	Superlative
good	better	best
bad	worse	worst
little	littler, less, lesser	littlest, least
many, some, much	more	most

Adverbs

Positive	Comparative	Superlative
well	better	best
badly	worse	worst

Comparative or Superlative?

In general, you will use the comparative form to compare two things; use the superlative form to compare three or more things.

> Twiskers was the **smarter** of the two hamsters.

> Marc was the **taller** of the two second-graders.

> Louisa is the **quicker** of the two runners.

> Of the six hamsters, Twiddles is the **smartest**.

> Among the six of you, Robert is the **tallest**.

> Of all the runners, Louisa is the **quickest**.

Double Comparisons

Do not use double comparatives or double superlatives.

> Amanda gets a bigger allowance because she is **older** (not *more older*) than I am.

> She is the **nicest** (not *most nicest*) girl in the class.

Completing Comparisons

Be careful not to omit words needed to complete comparisons.

> **Incomplete:**

> Steve's salary is **less than** his wife.

> **Complete:**

> Steve's salary is **less than** that of his wife.

or

Steve's salary is **less than** his wife's.

Incomplete:

Cooking with herbs is **more healthful than** fat.

Complete:

Cooking with herbs is **more healthful than** cooking with fat.

Incomplete:

Rainy days in Tucson are **as rare as** Santa Fe.

Complete:

Rainy days in Tucson are **as rare as** they are in Santa Fe.

Incomplete:

Denver is **farther from** Pueblo than Boulder.

Complete:

Denver is **farther from** Pueblo than it is from Boulder.

Incomplete:

New York City **has more** movie theaters.

Complete:

New York City **has more** movie theaters **than** any other city in the state.

Note: There are a number of words whose positive degree describes their only form.

Words such as *central*, *dead*, *empty*, *excellent*, *impossible*, *infinite*, *perfect*, *straight*, and *unique* cannot have a greater or lesser degree. Therefore, something cannot be *more unique* or *most infinite*.

In general, you should avoid using comparative or superlative forms for adjectives and adverbs that cannot be compared.

PREPOSITIONS

A *preposition* is a word used to connect and relate a noun or pronoun to some other word in the sentence.

COMMON PREPOSITIONS

about	besides	like
above	between	near
across	beyond	of
after	but	off
against	by	on
along	concerning	onto
amid	despite	opposite
among	down	out
around	during	outside
as	except	over
at	excepting	past
before	for	regarding
behind	from	round
below	in	since
beneath	inside	through
beside	into	throughout

till	underneath	with
to	until	within
toward	up	without
under	upon	

PHRASAL PREPOSITIONS (TWO OR MORE WORDS)

according to	in front of
along with	in lieu of
apart from	in place of
as for	in regard to
as of	in spite of
as regards	instead of
aside from	on account of
because of	out of
by means of	up to
by reason of	with reference to
by way of	with regard to
except for	with respect to
in addition to	with the exception of
in case of	

PREPOSITIONAL PHRASES

A preposition always has an object, which is a noun or pronoun. The preposition with its object and any modifiers is called a *prepositional phrase*. A prepositional phrase can be made up of any number of words:

toward the mountain

away from the ocean

by the side of the cliff

in front of the bushes

on account of his gross negligence

with the exception of three players

PLACEMENT OF PREPOSITIONS

A preposition usually precedes its object, but it may also follow its object. A preposition may also come at the end of the sentence:

What did Allison do that **for**?

Josh and Kate had many things to talk **about**.

For a week, she couldn't get the horrible scene **out of** her mind.

In addition to having a superb academic record, he was an outstanding athlete and humanitarian.

We know which chair you are hiding **behind**.

PREPOSITIONAL PHRASES AS ADVERBS AND ADJECTIVES

Prepositional phrases can function as adverbs or adjectives.

Prepositional Phrases as Adverbs

He hammered rapidly **underneath the overhang**.

The children flew their new dragon kite **on the beach**.

Charles drove **through the night**.

Prepositional Phrases as Adjectives

Melinda is the girl **with the missing front tooth**.

The reporter **in the red dress** asked the first question.

New York is a city that has something **for everyone**.

She was carrying a bag **of groceries**.

PREPOSITION OR ADVERB?

To distinguish between prepositions and adverbs, remember that prepositions, unlike adverbs, can never function alone within a sentence. A preposition must always have an object.

Prepositions

The children went **into** the house.

Crowds of people were skiing **down** the icy slopes.

Adverbs

They went **in**.

After the fifth book fell **down**, we decided it was time to rearrange the bookshelves.

CONJUNCTIONS

A *conjunction* is a word used to connect words, phrases, or clauses.

The three kinds of conjunctions are **coordinating**, **correlative**, and **subordinating**. Adverbs can also be used to link related ideas. When adverbs are used in this way, they are called *conjunctive adverbs*.

COORDINATING CONJUNCTIONS

A *coordinating conjunction* connects sentence parts (individual words, phrases, or clauses) of equal rank. Following are the most common coordinating conjunctions:

and	for	nor	yet
but	or	so	

And shows connections:

The children cleaned up quickly **and** quietly.

We went to a concert, **and** the children went to a movie.

But, nor, and *yet* show contrast:

The living room was extremely elegant **but** surprisingly comfortable.

My supervisor will never give us half days on Friday, **nor** will she agree to our other demands.

She took good care of the houseplant, **yet** it wilted and lost its leaves anyway.

Or shows choice:

You can have the spaghetti and meatballs **or** the veal and peppers.

We can have a picnic in the park, **or** we can drive out to the lake.

So shows result:

All the stores were closed, **so** we ended up eating peanut butter and jelly sandwiches.

For shows causality:

Laura stayed in the office late all week, **for** she had to finish the project by Friday.

CORRELATIVE CONJUNCTIONS

Correlative conjunctions also link sentence parts of equal grammatical rank. These conjunctions always work in pairs to connect words, phrases, or clauses.

both . . . and
either . . . or
neither . . . nor
not only . . . but also
not . . . but
whether . . . or

Both the bank **and** the post office are closed on national holidays.

Either you agree to ratify our contract now, **or** we will have to return to the bargaining table.

The envelopes are **neither** in the drawer **nor** in the cabinet.

Not only the children **but also** the adults were captivated by the dancing bears at the circus.

Not the renters **but** the homeowners were most deeply affected by the recent change in the tax laws.

Whether you agree to implement my plan **or** not, you have to concede that it has merit.

Note: The two elements connected by correlative conjunctions must be in parallel form.

Incorrect:

Neither the dripping cat **nor** the dog that was muddy was welcome in my foyer.

The hosts paid attention **not only** to the refreshments, **but** they **also** were paying attention to the music.

Correct:

Neither the dripping cat **nor** the muddy dog was welcome in my foyer.

The hosts paid attention **not only** to the refreshments **but also** to the music.

SUBORDINATING CONJUNCTIONS

A *subordinating conjunction* is a word that connects two thoughts by making one subordinate to, or dependent on, the other. To "subordinate" suggests making one statement less important than the other:

Although some people tried to repair the tennis courts, they were unable to gain sufficient public backing.

The main idea, "they were unable to gain sufficient public backing," is an independent clause (complete sentence); the subordinate idea, "Although some people tried to repair the tennis courts," is a dependent clause that functions here as an adverb. Either clause may come first in the sentence.

Common Subordinating Conjunctions

after	if	till
although	if only	unless
as	in order that	until
as long as	now that	when
as of	once	whenever
as soon as	rather than	where
as though	since	whereas
because	so that	wherever
before	than	while
even if	that	
even though	though	

Although traffic was light every morning, he was unable to arrive at work on time.

The little girl overheard her parents arguing in the next room **even though** they were whispering.

We ordered pizza **so that** we wouldn't have to go out in the rain.

Don't forget **that** your taxes are due on the fifteenth of the month.

Until you make up your mind, we won't be able to leave.

Please do the dishes **before** you go to the movies.

Do you know **where** he lives?

That is more **than** I can afford.

SUBORDINATING CONJUNCTION OR PREPOSITION?

A word such as *until*, *before*, *since*, *till*, or *after* can function as either a preposition or a subordinating conjunction. To distinguish between the two parts of speech, remember that subordinating conjunctions, unlike prepositions, connect two complete ideas.

Subordinating conjunctions

Please drop this tape off at the video store **since** you are driving in that direction anyway.

After you finish reading that book, may I borrow it?

Prepositions

I have had a headache **since** this morning.

After lunch I am going shopping **for** a new pair of shoes.

CONJUNCTIVE ADVERB OR TRANSITIONAL PHRASE?

A *conjunctive adverb* is an adverb that connects two clauses or sentences by describing their relationship to each other.

Common Conjunctive Adverbs

also	meanwhile
anyway	moreover
besides	nevertheless
consequently	next
finally	nonetheless
furthermore	otherwise
hence	still
however	then
incidentally	therefore
indeed	thus
instead	undoubtedly
likewise	

The electric company promised that power would be restored by tomorrow; **meanwhile**, we are using a generator.

The memo required an immediate response; **consequently**, we sent a fax.

You should not be angry at them for arriving early; **undoubtedly**, they were nervous and overestimated the time that the drive would take.

TRANSITIONAL PHRASE

Expressions that are used to link complete ideas are called *transitional phrases*.

Common Transitional Phrases

after all	for example
as a result	in addition
at any rate	in fact
at the same time	in other words
by the way	on the contrary
even so	on the other hand

The school building is in great disrepair; **for example**, the roof is leaking, the paint is peeling, and the heating system works erratically.

The voters rejected an increase in the school tax; **as a result**, the repairs will not be done this year.

There is a great public clamor for better schools; **at the same time**, no one wants to spend the necessary money.

Note: A semicolon is used before a conjunctive adverb or a transitional phrase that is placed between main clauses. The adverb or phrase itself is set off by a comma.

TRANSITIONAL PHRASE OR COORDINATING CONJUNCTION?

To distinguish between transitional phrases and coordinating conjunctions, ask yourself if the item can be moved. Conjunctive adverbs and transitional phrases can be moved within a sentence; coordinating conjunctions cannot:

> The taxi was late; however, we arrived in time to catch the entire first act.

> The taxi was late; we arrived, however, in time to catch the entire first act.

> The taxi was late; we arrived in time to catch the entire first act, however

INTERJECTIONS

An *interjection* is a word used to express strong emotion. It functions independently within a sentence.

In Latin, the word *interjection* means "something thrown in." In a sense, interjections are "thrown in" to add strong feeling.

For maximum effect, you should use interjections sparingly in your writing. Since they are independent from the rest of the sentence, they can be set off by commas or followed by an exclamation point.

Common Interjections

ah	darn	ouch
alas	hey	shh
bah	nonsense	well
bravo	oh	wow

Darn! The cat got out again.

Oh, I didn't expect you so early.

Hey! Do you know what you're doing?

PHRASES

A *phrase* is a group of related words that does not contain both a subject and a verb. Phrases are classified as **noun phrases, verb phrases, prepositional phrases**, and **verbal phrases** (participial phrases, gerund phrases, and infinitive phrases).

NOUN PHRASES

A *noun phrase* contains a noun and one or more modifiers.

The brilliant sunshine only made **the old house** look more dilapidated.

I have heard that she is **a very interesting speaker**.

A tall blue heron stood motionless on the shore.

VERB PHRASES

A *verb phrase* contains a main verb and an auxiliary verb.

The cat **has eaten** the carnations.

Let's go to the movies.

Can you **read** his handwriting?

PREPOSITIONAL PHRASES

A *prepositional phrase* is a group of words that opens with a preposition and ends with a noun or pronoun.

Prepositional phrases can function as adjectives, as adverbs, or, occasionally, as nouns.

Prepositional phrases used as adjectives

The price **of the dinner** was exorbitant.

My house is the one **between the twisted oak tree and the graceful weeping willow**.

Prepositional phrases used as adverbs

The joggers ran **with determination**.

My flight is scheduled to leave **at 6 P.M.**

Prepositional phrases used as nouns

After lunch is too late.

Beyond the oak tree is out of bounds.

VERBAL PHRASES

A *verbal* is a verb form used as another part of speech. Participles, infinitives, and gerunds are verbals. The verbal and all the words related to it are called a *verbal phrase*.

Participial phrases function as adjectives. They can be placed before or after the word they describe.

> **Shaking with fear,** the defendant stood before the jury. [present participle]

> She got a hot dog **drenched in mustard**. [past participle]

Gerund phrases function as nouns. Gerunds always end in *-ing*:

> **Swimming laps three times a week** helps her stay in shape.

> **Hiking in the Rockies** is my idea of a great vacation.

Infinitive phrases can function as nouns, adjectives, or adverbs. An infinitive phrase always begins with the word *to*:

> **To shop in that store** is a nightmare.
> [noun]

> We plan **to fly to Houston** on Monday.
> [noun]

> He gave us a lot of homework **to do**.
> [adjective]

> She struggled **to overcome** her disability.
> [adverb]

CLAUSES

A *clause* is a group of related words that contains both a subject and a verb. There are two types of clauses: **independent** (main) and **dependent** (subordinate).

INDEPENDENT CLAUSES

An *independent* (main) clause can stand alone as a complete sentence.

> Swimming is suitable for people of all ages.
> He missed his train.
> Marcia plans to open a catering business.

DEPENDENT CLAUSES

A *dependent* (subordinate) clause functions as a part of speech that relates to an element in the main clause.

Swimming, **which is very good exercise**, is suitable for people of all ages.

Because he overslept, he missed his train.

Marcia, **who won the blue ribbon in the cooking contest**, plans to open a catering business.

Functions of Dependent Clauses

A dependent clause functions as a part of speech—as an adjective, an adverb, or a noun.

ADJECTIVE CLAUSES

An *adjective clause* is a subordinate clause that modifies a noun or pronoun. It usually begins with a relative pronoun: *which, what, whatever, who, whose, whom, whoever, whomever,* or *that*. It may also begin with words such as *when, where, before, since,* or *why*. An adjective clause almost always follows the word it modifies:

We hired the candidates **who came with the strongest recommendations**.

The child **whom you saw in the magazine** is my niece.

Did Fred tell you the reason **why he was late for work this morning**?

Good restaurants **where one can eat cheaply** are very rare in this town.

ADVERB CLAUSES

An *adverb clause* is a subordinate clause that modifies a verb, an adjective, an adverb, or a verbal. Adverb clauses usually begin with subordinating conjunctions (See page 65 for a list of subordinating conjunctions). Unlike adjective clauses, adverb clauses can be separated from the word they modify and can be placed anywhere in the sentence. If the clause is placed at the beginning or in the middle of a sentence, it is often set off by commas.

Since the guests were so convivial, I soon forgot my troubles.

Did you visit the Metropolitan Museum **when you were in New York**?

I decided, **after I lost an important document,** to make backup copies of all my files.

NOUN CLAUSES

A *noun clause* is a subordinate clause that acts as a noun. Noun clauses can function as subjects, objects, and predicate nouns within sentences. They begin either with a relative pronoun or with a word such as *how, why, where, when, if,* or *whether.*

Noun clauses can be difficult to identify. Since so many different words can be used to begin a noun clause, you cannot decide on the basis of the opening word alone. You must discover the function of the clause within the sentence to identify it as a noun clause.

Whoever washes the dishes will be allowed to choose which program to watch. [subject]

Do you know **where they went on vacation**? [direct object]

They talked about **whether they could take the time off from work**. [object of a preposition]

That is **what I meant**. [predicate nominative]

ELLIPTICAL CLAUSES

An *elliptical clause* is a subordinate clause that is grammatically incomplete but nonetheless clear because the missing element can be understood from the rest of the sentence. The word *elliptical* comes from *ellipsis*, which means "omission." The verb from the second part of the comparison may be missing, or the relative pronouns *that*, *which*, and *whom* may be omitted from adjectival clauses. Often, elliptical clauses begin with *as* or *than*, although any subordinating conjunction that makes logical sense can be used. In the following examples, the omitted words are supplied in parentheses:

Chad's younger cousin is as tall as he (**is**).

Aruba is among the islands (**that**) they visited on their recent cruise.

When (**he was**) only a child, Barry was taken on a tour around the world.

Although (**they were**) common fifty years ago, passenger pigeons are extinct today.

SENTENCES

SUBJECTS AND PREDICATES

There are two basic parts to every sentence: the **subject** and the **predicate**.

The simple subject is the noun or pronoun that identifies the person, place, or thing the sentence is about. The complete subject is the simple subject and all the words that modify it.

The predicate contains the verb that explains what the subject is doing. The simple predicate contains only the verb; the complete predicate contains the verb and any complements and modifiers.

Subject	Predicate
The motorcycle	veered away from the boulder.
Calico cats	are always female.
One of Hawthorne's direct blood relatives	was the famous "hanging judge" of the Salem witchcraft trials.
Farmingdale, in the town of Oyster Bay,	has recently begun a massive recycling project.

HARD-TO-LOCATE SUBJECTS

COMMANDS OR DIRECTIONS

In some instances, the subject can be difficult to locate. In commands or directions, for instance, the subject is often not stated because it is understood to be *you*.

Subject	Predicate
(you)	Please unload the dishwasher and tidy the kitchen.
(you)	Just tell me what happened that evening.

QUESTIONS

In questions, too, subjects can be difficult to locate because they often follow the verb rather than come before it. Rewriting the question as a statement will make it easier to find the subject.

Question:

Are **you** planning to go to Oregon this weekend or next?

Rewritten as a statement:

You are planning to go to Oregon this weekend or next.

SENTENCES BEGINNING WITH *THERE* OR *HERE*

If you are having trouble locating the subject of a sentence beginning with *there* or *here*, try rephrasing the sentence:

There is **your wallet** on the table.

Here are **the peaches** from the farm market.

Rewritten:

Your wallet is there on the table.

The peaches from the farm market are here.

INVERTED SENTENCES

Inverted sentences place the subject after the verb for emphasis.

High on the cliff above the ocean stood **the diver**.

On a rack behind the door hung **a dripping raincoat**.

Even more significant was **the lack of a firm objective**.

SENTENCE COMPLEMENTS

Along with a verb, complete predicates may contain a complement. A *complement* is a word or word group that completes the meaning of the verb.

There are four primary kinds of sentence complements: **direct objects**, **indirect objects**, **object complements**, and **subject complements** (nouns, pronouns, and adjectives).

DIRECT OBJECTS

A *direct object* is the noun, pronoun, or word acting as a noun that completes the meaning of a transitive verb by receiving the action. (Intransitive verbs do not have direct objects.) To help decide if a word is a direct object, ask *What?* or *Whom?* after an action verb:

Martha won **the stuffed dog**.
(What did she win? *The stuffed dog.*)

The hurricane destroyed **the beach and the boardwalk**.
(What did the hurricane destroy? *The beach and the boardwalk.*)

The waiter served **Jack**.
(Whom did the waiter serve? *Jack.*)

INDIRECT OBJECTS

An *indirect object* is a noun or pronoun that names the person or thing that something is done to or given to. Indirect objects are located after the verb and before the direct object. They are found only in sentences that have direct objects. Indirect objects answer the questions *To whom? For whom? To what?* or *For what?*

My aunt lent **me** her motorcycle.
(To whom did my aunt lend her motorcycle? *To me.*)

I gave **my daughter** a computer for her birthday.
(To whom did I give a computer. *To my daughter.*)

Maria sent **Serge** an invitation.
(To whom did Maria send an invitation? *To Serge.*)

OBJECT COMPLEMENTS

An *object complement* is a noun or adjective immediately following a direct object. It either renames or describes the direct object.

She called him **a fool**.

We made the platypus **our mascot**.

They named the kitten **Ivan the Terrible**.

SUBJECT COMPLEMENTS

Subject complements, like object complements, are found in the predicate of a sentence.

A *subject complement* is a noun, pronoun, or adjective that follows a linking verb and gives further information about the subject of a sentence.

A predicate noun or pronoun follows a linking verb to identify the subject of a sentence:

The new head of the division will be **Elizabeth Fabian**.

Which of those two phones is **the newer one**?

A predicate adjective follows a linking verb to describe the subject of a sentence:

The vegetable soup smells **delicious**.

My daughter's stamp collection grows **larger** and **more valuable** every day.

FORMING SENTENCES

Independent and dependent clauses can be combined in various ways to create four basic types of sentences: **simple**, **compound**, **complex**, and **compound-complex**.

SIMPLE SENTENCES

A *simple sentence* is one independent clause, a group of words containing one subject and one predicate. This does not mean, however, that a simple sentence must be short. Both the subject and the verb may be compounded. In addition, a simple sentence may contain describing phrases. By definition, though, a simple sentence cannot have a subordinate clause or another independent clause.

Heather shopped.

The carpenter and the electrician arrived simultaneously.

The shingle flapped, folded, and broke off.

Either my mother or my grandmother bought and wrapped this lovely crystal decanter.

Freezing unexpectedly, the water in the copper lines burst the gaskets.

COMPOUND SENTENCES

A *compound sentence* is two or more independent clauses joined together. Since the clauses in a compound sentence are independent, each can be written as an individual sentence. A compound sentence does not have dependent clauses. The independent clauses can be connected by a comma and a coordinating conjunction (*and*, *but*, *or*, *for*, *so*, *yet*) or by a semicolon. If the clauses are very short, the comma before the coordinating conjunction may be omitted.

Mary went to the concert, but Bill stayed home with the baby.

You may mail the enclosed form back to our central office, or you may call our customer service representative at the number listed above.

Eddie typed the report in three hours; Donna spent five hours editing it.

I ate lunch and then I took a nap.

COMPLEX SENTENCES

A *complex sentence* contains one independent clause and one or more subordinate clauses. To distinguish it from the other clauses, the independent clause in a complex sentence is called the main clause. In a complex sentence, each clause has its own subject and verb. The subject in the main clause is called the subject of the sentence; the verb in the main clause is called the main verb. An independent clause can stand alone as a complete sentence; a dependent clause cannot.

In the following examples, the main clauses are in boldface type.

As we were looking over your sign-in sheets for May and June, **we noticed a number of minor problems**.

While Mary went to the concert, **Bill stayed home with the baby**.

No one responded when she rang the front doorbell.

The owners of the small mountain inns rejoiced when the snow fell

COMPOUND-COMPLEX SENTENCES

A *compound-complex sentence* has at least two independent clauses and at least one dependent clause. The compound-complex sentence is so named because it shares the characteristics of both compound and complex sentences. Like the compound sentence, the compound-complex has at least two main clauses. Like the complex sentence, it has at least one subordinate clause. The subordinate clause can be part of an independent clause.

In the following examples, the main clauses are in boldface type.

> Since my memo seems to outline our requirements fully, **we are circulating it to all the departments; please notify us** if we can be of any further assistance.

> When the heat comes, **the lakes dry up**, and **farmers know that their crops will fail**.

REVIEW OF SENTENCE FORMS

The following five sentence forms are the basic templates on which all sentences are built.

1. Subject + intransitive verb
    Bond prices fell.

2. Subject + transitive verb + direct object

Bobbie hummed the song.

3. Subject + transitive verb + direct object + object complement

   The committee appointed Eric secretary.

4. Subject + linking verb + subject complement

   The procedure was tedious.

   The gift was a silk scarf.

5. Subject + transitive verb + indirect object + direct object

   The clerk gave us the receipt.

SENTENCE FUNCTIONS

In addition to the form they take, sentences can also be classified according to function. There are four main types of sentences: **declarative**, **interrogative**, **imperative**, and **exclamatory**.

DECLARATIVE SENTENCES

A *declarative sentence* makes a statement and always ends with a period:

   On Thursday we are going to see a movie.

   We have been waiting for two weeks for the movie to open here.

   The reviews were excellent.

INTERROGATIVE SENTENCES

An *interrogative sentence* asks a question and always ends with a question mark:

Are we going to see the movie on
Tuesday?

How long have you been waiting for
the movie to open?

What did the reviewers say about it?

IMPERATIVE SENTENCES

An *imperative sentence* makes a command.
In many instances, the subject of an imperative sentence is understood to be *you* and is
thus not stated. In other instances, the sentence may be phrased as a question but does
not end with a question mark.

Take this money in case you change your
mind.

Clean up that mess!

Will you please reply at your earliest
convenience.

Would someone please move those books
to the top shelf.

EXCLAMATORY SENTENCES

An *exclamatory sentence* conveys strong feeling and always ends with an exclamation
point. Many exclamatory sentences are very
strongly stated declarative sentences. Since
the exclamatory sentence conveys strong
emotions, it is not found much in formal
writing.

They still haven't called!

The dress is ruined!

SENTENCE ERRORS

Sentence errors fall into three main divisions: parts of sentences set off as though they were complete (**fragments**), two or more sentences incorrectly joined (**run-ons**), and sentence parts misplaced or poorly connected to the rest of the sentence (**misplaced, dangling,** or **squinting modifiers**).

FRAGMENTS

A *fragment* is part of a sentence presented as though it were a complete sentence. The fragment may lack a subject or verb or both, or it may be a subordinate clause not connected to a complete sentence. Since fragments are not complete sentences, they do not express complete thoughts.

No subject:

Ran to catch the bus.

Ate all the chocolate hidden in the drawer.

No main verb:

The box sitting in the trunk.

The man in the room.

No subject or main verb:

Feeling happy.

Acting poorly.

Subordinate clause:

When I woke him up early this morning.

If it is as pleasant as you expect today.

Correcting Fragments

Fragments are often created when phrases and subordinate clauses are punctuated as though they were complete sentences. Remember that phrases can never stand alone because they are groups of words that do not have subjects or verbs. To correct phrase fragments, add the information they need to be complete.

Subordinate clauses, on the other hand, do contain subjects and verbs. Like phrases, however, they do not convey complete thoughts. You can complete them by connecting them to main clauses. They can also be completed by dropping the subordinating conjunction. Correct each fragment in the way that makes the most logical sense within the context of the passage.

Phrase fragment:

a big house

Corrected:

A big house at the end of the block burned down last night.

(Fragment becomes subject; predicate is added.)

My sister recently bought a big house.

(Fragment becomes direct object; subject and verb are added.)

She earned enough money for a big house.

(Fragment becomes object of the preposition; subject, verb, and direct object are added.)

Did you hear about his newest acquisition, the big house on Maple Street?

(Fragment becomes appositive; subject, verb, and prepositional phrase are added.)

Subordinating clause fragment:

If it is as pleasant as you expected today.

Corrected:

It is as pleasant as you expected today.

(Subordinating conjunction dropped.)

If it is as pleasant as you expected today, we will be able to go to the beach.

(Fragment connected to a main clause.)

RUN-ONS

A *run-on* is two complete ideas incorrectly joined. Run-ons are generally classified as either comma splices or fused sentences. A *comma splice* incorrectly joins two independent clauses with a comma.

Mary walked into the room, she found a mouse on her desk.

The vest was beautiful, it had intricate embroidery.

My daughter loves *Buffy the Vampire Slayer*, she watches it every week.

A *fused sentence* runs two independent clauses together without an appropriate conjunction or punctuation mark:

Many people are afraid of computers they do not realize how easy it is to learn basic tasks.

All the word processing programs come with built-in lessons you can learn to do basic word processing in an afternoon or less.

The on-line spell checker and thesaurus are especially handy they do not take the place of a good dictionary.

Correcting Run-on Sentences

There are four ways to correct both comma splices and fused sentences.

1. Separate the clauses into two sentences.

   Mary walked into the room. She found a mouse on her desk.

   Many people are afraid of computers. They do not realize how easy it is to learn basic tasks.

2. Insert a comma and coordinating conjunction between clauses to create a compound sentence.

   Mary walked into the room, and she found a mouse on her desk.

   Many people are afraid of computers, for they do not realize how easy it is to learn basic tasks.

3. Insert a semicolon between the clauses.

   Mary walked into the room; she found a mouse on her desk.

   Many people are afraid of computers; they do not realize how easy it is to learn basic tasks.

Sentences **89**

4. Subordinate one clause to the other to create a complex sentence.

When Mary walked into the room, she found a mouse on her desk.

Many people are afraid of computers because they do not realize how easy it is to learn basic tasks.

MISPLACED MODIFIERS

A *misplaced modifier* occurs when the modifier looks as if it is describing the wrong word in the sentence.

As a general rule, a modifier should be placed as close as possible to the word it modifies. When a word, phrase, or clause is placed too far from the word it modifies, the sentence may fail to convey the intended meaning and therefore produce ambiguity or amusement. When this occurs, the modifier is called *misplaced*.

Words misplaced:

To get to the ski slope we **nearly** drove five hours.

I **almost** drank a whole quart of water.

Revised:

To get to the ski slope we drove **nearly** five hours.

I drank **almost** a whole quart of water.

Phrases misplaced:

We all stared at the woman who was talking to the governor **with green spiked hair**.

Roasted whole, those who shied away from garlic will delight in this new vegetable.

The professor explained how her grading system worked **on Monday**.

Revised:

We all stared at the woman **with green spiked hair** who was talking to the governor.

Those who shied away from garlic will delight in this new vegetable when it is **roasted whole**.

On Monday the professor explained how her grading system worked.

Clauses misplaced:

I bought Brie in the new shop on North Road **that cost $8.00 a pound**.

We saved the balloons for the children **that had been left on the table**.

Revised:

I bought Brie **that cost $8.00 a pound** in the new shop on North Road.

We saved the balloons **that had been left on the table** for the children.

DANGLING MODIFIERS

A *dangling modifier,* also called an unattached modifier, occurs when a modifier does not logically or grammatically describe anything in the sentence because the noun or pronoun to which a phrase or clause refers is either in the wrong place or missing. Like misplaced modifiers, dangling modifiers cause confusion.

Examples of dangling modifiers:

While reading the paper, the birds on the railing caught my eye.

Biking up the hill, a Jaguar went roaring past.

Drinking a cup of coffee, the cat leaped on the table.

The evening passed contentedly, reading and listening to music.

Sitting on the riverbank, the sun glinted on the rippling waves.

After closing the door, the room got very warm.

In planning a European trip, consideration of the amount of luggage is needed.

To graduate with honors, exceptional ability and hard work are needed.

When travelling, my passport is in my inside pocket.

Revised:

While I was reading the paper, the birds on the railing caught my eye.

As I was biking up the hill, a Jaguar went roaring past.

While I was drinking a cup of coffee, the cat leaped on the table.

We passed the evening contentedly, reading and listening to music.

Sitting on the riverbank, I watched the sun glinting on the rippling waves.

After I had closed the door, the room got very warm.

In planning a European trip, one needs to consider the amount of luggage one can carry.

To graduate with honors, one needs exceptional ability and hard work.

When travelling, I carry my passport in my inside pocket.

Or

When I am travelling, my passport is in my inside pocket.

SQUINTING MODIFIERS

A *squinting modifier* is one that may refer to either a preceding or following word and therefore causes ambiguity and confusion.

Examples of squinting modifiers:

We said **when we were coming back from the Cape** that we would like to buy some local produce.

Exercising **often** gives me energy.

The case that the prosecution had prepared **quickly** forced it to declare the defendant's sister a hostile witness.

Revised:

We said we would like to buy some local produce **when we were coming back from the Cape**.

Or

When we were coming back from the Cape, we said we would like to buy some local produce.

Often, exercising gives me energy.

Or

It gives me energy to exercise **often**.

The case that the prosecution had **quickly** prepared forced it to declare the defendant's sister a hostile witness.

Or

The case that the prosecution had prepared forced it to **quickly** declare the defendant's sister a hostile witness.

AGREEMENT OF SENTENCE PARTS

Agreement is what it sounds like—matching. Specifically, agreement refers to the matching of number, person, and gender within a sentence. Subjects and verbs must agree in number (singular or plural) and person (first, second, or third). Pronouns and their antecedents (the words to which they refer) must also match in gender (masculine, feminine, or neuter).

Sentences that do not maintain agreement among all their elements sound clumsy and can be ambiguous.

SUBJECT-VERB AGREEMENT

A subject must agree with its verb in number. A singular subject takes a singular verb. A plural subject takes a plural verb.

First, find the subject; then determine whether it is singular or plural. The subject is the noun or pronoun that is doing the action. Often, it will be located at the beginning of the sentence, as in the following example:

I **recommend** that company highly.

Here, the subject *I* is doing the action *recommend*.

Sometimes the subject will follow the verb, as in questions and in sentences beginning with *here* and *there*. In the following example, the verb *are* comes before the subject *roads*:

There **are two roads** you can take.

The same is true of the placement of the subject and verb in the following question, as the verb "is" comes before the subject *briefcase*:

Where **is your briefcase**?

After you have located the subject, decide whether it is singular or plural. In English, confusion can arise because most present-tense verbs add *-s* or *-es* when their subject is third-person singular (He *runs* fast. She *studies* a lot.), whereas nouns ending in *-s* or *-es* are plural (*potatoes*, *computers*). The following table shows how regular English verbs are conjugated in the present tense:

Singular	**Plural**
I dream	we dream
you dream	you dream
he, she, it dreams	they dream

There are a number of plural nouns that are regarded as singular in meaning, as well as other nouns that can be both singular and plural, depending on the context of the sentence. *Acoustics*, *athletics*, *economics*, *gymnastics*, *mathematics*, *physics*, *politics*, and *statistics*, for example, are often treated as singular nouns.

Acoustics is the branch of physics that deals with sound.

The acoustics in the new hall **are** excellent.

Gymnastics is an Olympic sport.

Verbal gymnastics are his forte.

Statistics is the science that deals with the collection and analysis of numerical data.

The statistics show that the town's population has increased by twenty-two percent in the past decade.

Often, a phrase or clause will intervene between a subject and a verb. These intervening words should not affect subject-verb agreement, as illustrated in the following examples.

The supervisor of the department, together with her sales force, **is taking** the 8:30 shuttle to Washington.

The deputies to the mayor **are** exploring alternate methods of disposing of newspapers.

A display of luscious foods sometimes **encourages** impulse buying.

The profits earned this quarter **are** much higher than we had expected.

Singular subjects connected by *or, nor, either . . . or*, or *neither . . . nor* take a singular verb if both subjects are singular, a plural verb if both subjects are plural.

Either your supervisor or your colleague has to take responsibility for the error.

Either supervisors or colleagues have to take responsibility for the error.

Neither the sled nor the snow shovel has been put away.

Either the clown or the magician is scheduled to appear at the library on Sunday afternoon.

Neither boots nor shoes are included in the one-day sale.

If a subject consists of both singular and plural nouns or pronouns connected by *or* or *nor*, the verb usually agrees with the closer noun or pronoun.

In the following sentence, the plural verb *want* agrees with the plural noun *students*:

Neither the teacher nor the students want to be here.

Notice that the verb becomes singular when *teacher* and *students* are reversed:

Neither the students nor the teacher wants to be here.

This is one rule of thumb. For many people, the presence of one plural subject, no matter what its position, signals the use of a plural verb. Either method is correct; however, your writing must be consistent. Choose one of these rules and stick with it. Some writers place the plural subject closer to the verb to avoid awkwardness:

Neither we nor she has distributed the memo yet.

Neither she nor we have distributed the memo yet.

Either Martha, Ruth, or the Champney girls are planning to organize the graduation party.

Two or more subjects, phrases, or clauses connected by *and* take a plural verb. Whether the individual subjects are singular or plural, together they form a compound subject, which is plural:

The president and her advisers were behind schedule.

The faculty and staff have planned a joint professional retreat.

Derek and his dog jog before work every morning.

Sleeping late Sunday morning and reading the paper help me relax after a long week at work.

Traditionally, when the subjects joined by *and* refer to the same object or person or stand for a single idea, the entire subject is treated as a unit. Most often, the personal pronoun or article before the parts of the compound subject indicates whether the subject is indeed seen as a unit. As with other matters of agreement, this varies widely in actual use:

Unit as singular:

Ham and Swiss is my favorite sandwich.

(*Ham and Swiss* is treated as a type of sandwich.)

My mentor and friend guides me through difficult career decisions.

(*Mentor* and *friend* are the same person.)

Unit as plural:

Ham and Swiss make a great sandwich.

(Each ingredient is treated as separate.)

My mentor and my friend guide me through difficult career decisions.

(*Mentor* and *friend* are two different people.)

Mixed units:

Ham and eggs was once considered a nutritious and healthful breakfast; now, **cereal and fresh fruit are** considered preferable.

Nouns that refer to weight, extent, time, fractions, portions, or amount considered as one unit usually take a singular verb; those that indicate separate units usually take a plural verb.

In the first two examples below, the subjects are considered as single units and therefore take a singular verb. In the last two, the subjects are considered as individual items and therefore take a plural verb.

Seventy-five cents is more than enough to buy what you want at the penny carnival.

Three-fourths of the harvest was saved through their heroic efforts.

Half of the nails were rusted.

Fifty pounds of homegrown tomatoes are being divided among the eager shoppers.

Collective Nouns

Collective nouns (nouns that are singular in form but denote a group of persons or objects) may be either singular or plural, depending on the meaning of the sentence.

Common Collective Nouns

assembly	couple	minority
association	crowd	number
audience	family	pair
board	flock	part
class	group	percent
commission	half	press
committee	herd	public
company	jury	series
corporation	legion	staff
council	majority	

You should determine agreement for each collective noun on a sentence-by-sentence basis. If the sentence implies that the group named by the collective noun acts as a single unit, use a singular verb. If the sentence implies that the group named by the collective noun acts individually, use a plural verb.

The budget committee is voting on a new accountant this week.

The budget committee are in complete disagreement about the choice of a new accountant.

The team are trying on their new game jerseys.

The jury, not the judge, **makes** the final decision.

Gotthelf & Company is hosting its annual holiday party this Friday evening.

The phrases *the number* and *the total* are usually singular, but the phrases *a number* and *a total* are usually plural:

The number of new members is astonishing.

A number of new members were at the meeting.

When the collective nouns *couple* and *pair* refer to people, they are usually treated as plurals:

The pair are hosting a New Year's open house.

The couple have bought a large apartment with a view of the river.

Note: In British English, a collective noun naming an organization regarded as a unit is usually treated as plural:

Gotthelf & Company are hosting their annual holiday party this Friday evening.

The team have eight games scheduled for September.

PRONOUN-ANTECEDENT AGREEMENT

A pronoun must agree with its antecedent— the word to which the pronoun refers—in number and gender.

Traditionally, certain indefinite pronouns were always considered singular, some were always considered plural, and some could be both singular and plural. As language changes, however, many of these rules are changing. *None*, for example, was tradition- ally treated as a singular pronoun even though it has been used with both singular and plural verbs since the ninth century. Today when the sense is "not any persons or things," the plural is more commonly used:

The rescue party searched for survivors, but **none were** found.

When *none* is clearly intended to mean "not one" or "not any," it is followed by a singular verb:

Of all my court cases, **none has been** more stressful than yours.

None of us is going to the concert.

The following lists, therefore, are presented as general guidelines, not hard-and-fast rules. In general, use singular verbs with indefinite pronouns.

Indefinite pronouns that are most often considered singular

anybody	everybody	nothing
anyone	everyone	one
anything	everything	somebody
each	many a	someone
either	neither	
every	nobody	

Indefinite pronouns that are always considered plural

both	many	several
few	others	

Indefinite pronouns that can be considered singular or plural

all	more	none
any	most	some

Each of the people observes all the safety regulations.

Few are comfortable during a job interview.

Some of the water is seeping into the wall, but **most of the files remain** dry.

All the food has been donated to charity.

All the children have had cake and ice cream.

The effort to avoid the sexist implications of *he* has led to the general acceptance, in informal speech and writing, of *they*, *their*, and *them* to refer to indefinite pronouns:

Everyone began putting on **their** coats.

If **anybody** calls, tell **them** I'll call back after 10:00.

In formal speech and writing, *he* or *she* is still preferred to refer to indefinite pronouns.

Everyone handed in **his** test.

Anyone who wants **her** children to succeed will stress the importance of education to them.

SHIFTS

A *shift* is an unnecessary or illogical change of tense, voice, mood, person, number, tone or style, viewpoint, or direct and indirect quotations within a sentence, paragraph, or essay. Shifts confuse your reader and distort the meaning of your writing.

SHIFTS IN TENSE

A shift in *tense* occurs when the tenses of verbs within a sentence or paragraph do not logically match.

Confusing:

Throughout the eighties the junk-bond market **rose** steadily; as a result, small investors **invest** heavily from 1985 to 1989.

Revised:

Throughout the eighties the junk-bond market **rose** steadily; as a result, small investors **invested** heavily from 1985 to 1989.

Confusing:

Last night I **was watching** my favorite television show. Suddenly the show **is interrupted** for a special news bulletin. I **lean forward** and **will** eagerly **watch** the screen for information.

Revised:

Last night I **was watching** my favorite television show. Suddenly the show **was**

interrupted for a special news bulletin. I **leaned forward** and eagerly **watched** the screen for information.

Note: If you are using the present tense to narrate events in a literary work, be careful not to slip into the past tense.

SHIFTS IN VOICE

Voice shows whether the subject of the verb acts or is acted upon. (See page 42.) When the subject of the verb does the action, the sentence is said to be in the *active voice:*

Dave hit a home run.

When the subject of the verb receives the action, the sentence is said to be in the *passive voice:*

The home run was hit by Dave.

You should avoid changing from active voice to passive voice within a sentence.

Confusing:

As **we finished** our coffee, **the servers were seen** clearing the adjacent tables.

Revised:

As **we finished** our coffee, **we saw** the servers clearing the adjacent tables.

Confusing:

The cook mixed the bread dough until it was blended, and then **it was set** in the warm oven to rise.

Revised:

The cook mixed the bread dough until it was blended and then **set** it in the warm oven to rise.

Or

The bread dough was mixed until it was blended, and then **it was set** in the warm oven to rise.

SHIFTS IN MOOD

The *mood* of a verb indicates the manner in which it is used. English has three moods: **indicative**, **subjunctive**, and **imperative**. (See page 40.)

Confusing:

Stroke the paint on evenly, but **you should not** dab it on corners and edges. [Shift from imperative to indicative]

Revised:

Stroke the paint on evenly, but **don't dab** it on corners and edges.

Or

You should stroke the paint on evenly, but **you shouldn't dab** it on corners and edges.

Confusing:

The cleaning service **asked** that they get better hours and **they want** to work fewer weekends as well. [Shift from subjunctive to indicative]

Revised:

The cleaning service **asked** that they get better hours and that they work fewer weekends as well.

Or

The cleaning service **asked** to work better hours and fewer weekends.

Or

The cleaning service **wants** to work better hours and fewer weekends.

Confusing:

If the rain **stopped** and the sun **comes out**, we **could have** a picnic. [Shift from subjunctive to indicative]

Revised:

If the rain **stopped** and the sun **came** out, we **could have** a picnic.

Or

If the rain **stops** and the sun **comes** out, we **can have** a picnic.

SHIFTS IN PERSON

Person is the form a pronoun or verb takes to show the person or persons speaking: the first person (*I, we*), the second person (*you*), or the third person (*he, she, it, they*). As the pronouns indicate, the first person is the person speaking, the second person is the person spoken to, and the third person is the person, concept, or thing spoken about.

Shifts between second- and third-person pronouns cause the most confusion. The following examples illustrate common shifts in person and different ways to revise such shifts.

Confusing:

When **one** shops for an automobile, **you** should research various models in consumer magazines and read all the advertisements as well as speak to salespeople. [Shift from the third to the second person]

Revised:

When **you** shop for an automobile, **you** should research various models in consumer magazines and read all the advertisements as well as speak to salespeople.

Or

When **one** shops for an automobile, **one** should research various models in consumer magazines and read all the advertisements as well as speak to salespeople.

Or

When **people** shop for an automobile, **they** should research various models in consumer magazines and read all the advertisements as well as speak to salespeople.

Confusing:

When **a person** applies themselves diligently, **you** can accomplish a surprising amount.

Revised:

When **people** apply themselves diligently, **they** can accomplish a surprising amount.

Or

When **you** apply yourself diligently, **you** can accomplish a surprising amount.

Or

When **a person** applies himself or herself diligently, **he or she** can accomplish a surprising amount.

SHIFTS IN PERSPECTIVE

Shifts in *perspective* are related to shifts in person that change the vantage point from which a story is told. As with other shifts, there will be occasions when it is desirable to shift perspective; however, unnecessary shifts confuse readers. In the following example, the perspective shifts from above the water to below without adequate transition.

Confusing:

The frothy surface of the ocean danced with bursts of light, and the fish swam lazily through the clear water and waving plants.

Revised:

The frothy surface of the ocean danced with bursts of light; below, the fish swam lazily through the clear water and waving plants.

SHIFTS IN NUMBER

Number indicates one (singular) or more than one (plural). Shifts in number occur with nouns and personal pronouns because both change form to show differences in number. Confusion with number occurs especially often between a pronoun and its antecedent and between words whose meanings relate to each other. Remember to use singular pronouns to refer to singular antecedents and plural pronouns to refer to plural antecedents.

Confusing:

If **a person** does not keep up with household chores, **they** will find that things pile up with alarming speed.

Revised:

If **a person** does not keep up with household chores, **he or she** will find that things pile up with alarming speed.

Or

If **people** do not keep up with household chores, **they** will find that things pile up with alarming speed.

Confusing:

All the repair stations have **a good reputation**.

Revised:

All the repair stations have **good reputations**.

PERSON AND NUMBER WITH COLLECTIVE NOUNS

Maintaining consistency of person and number is especially tricky with collective nouns since many can be either singular or plural, depending on the context. Once you establish a collective noun as singular or plural within a sentence, maintain consistency throughout.

Confusing:

Because **my company** bases **their** bonus on amount of income generated yearly, we must all do our share to enable **it** to give a generous bonus.

Revised:

Because **my company** bases **its** bonus on amount of income generated yearly, we must all do our share to enable **it** to give a generous bonus.

Or

Because **my company** bases **their** bonus on amount of income generated yearly, we must all do our share to enable **them** to give a generous bonus.

Confusing:

The jury is divided on whether or not **they** should demand additional evidence.

Revised:

The jury are divided on whether or not **they** should demand additional evidence. [Jury functioning as separate individuals]

SHIFTS IN TONE AND STYLE

Tone is the writer's attitude toward his or her readers and subject. As pitch and volume convey tone in speaking, so word choice and sentence structure help convey tone in writing. Tone can be formal or informal, humorous or earnest, distant or friendly, pompous or personal. Obviously, different tones are appropriate for different audiences.

Style is a writer's way of writing. Style comprises every way a writer uses language. Elements of style include tone, word choice, figurative language, grammatical structure, rhythm, and sentence length and organization.

A piece of writing is more powerful and effective if consistent tone and style are maintained throughout.

Shift:

Reporters who assert that freedom of the press can be maintained without judicial intervention are out of their minds. [Shift from elevated diction to colloquial]

Revised:

Reporters who assert that freedom of the press can be maintained without judicial intervention are greatly mistaken.

Shift:

Their leavetaking was marked by the same affability that had characterized their entire visit with us. Later, we discussed what cool dudes they were. [Shift from standard English to colloquial]

Revised:

Their leavetaking was marked by the same affability that had characterized their entire visit with us. Later, we discussed their good humor, consideration, and generosity.

SHIFTS IN DIRECT AND INDIRECT QUOTATIONS

Direct quotations use quotation marks to report a speaker's exact words: "I'll be the referee for today's game," Ms. Marin said. Usually, direct quotations are also marked by a phrase such as *she said* or *he remarked*, which indicates the speaker.

Indirect quotations report what was said, but not necessarily in the speaker's own words: Ms. Marin said that she would be the referee for today's game. Since the remarks do not have to be reproduced exactly, indirect quotations do not use quotation marks. Often, a reported statement will be introduced by *that*, *who*, *how*, *if*, *what*, *when*, or *whether*.

Illogical shifts between direct and indirect quotations can become wordy and confuse readers. As the following examples show, these errors can usually be eliminated by recording a speaker's remarks with logic and consistency regardless of whether you choose to use direct quotations, indirect quotations, or a combination of the two.

Wordy:

Poet and critic T. S. Eliot said that he feels that the progress of an artist was like a long process of sacrifice of self, "a continual extinction of personality."

Revised:

Poet and critic T. S. Eliot said that the progress of an artist was like a long process of self-sacrifice, "a continual extinction of personality."

Or

Poet and critic T. S. Eliot said that to progress, artists must sacrifice and extinguish the self.

Confusing:

Jill asked whether we had cut down the storm-damaged tree and was there any further damage.

Revised:

Jill asked whether we had cut down the storm-damaged tree and if there was any further damage.

Or

Jill asked, "Did you cut down the tree damaged by the storm? Was there any further damage?"

Confusing:

My son said he was very busy and would I please take the cat to the vet.

Revised:

My son said he was very busy and asked if I would take the cat to the vet.

PARALLELISM

Parallel Structure

Parallelism, or parallel structure, means that grammatical elements that share the same function will share the same form. Parallel structure ensures that ideas of equal rank are expressed in similar ways and that separate word groups appear in the same grammatical forms.

Individual words, phrases, clauses, or sentences can be paralleled. For example, adjectives are paired with adjectives, and verbs correspond with matching verbs in tense, mood, voice, and number. Parallel structure helps coordinate ideas and strengthen logic and symmetry.

Study the following pairs of examples. Note how much more smoothly the sentences flow when the constructions are parallel.

Not parallel:

Lindsy was hot, cranky, and needed food.

Parallel:

Lindsy was hot, cranky, and hungry.

Not parallel:

Sam is organized, efficient, and works hard.

Parallel:

Sam is organized, efficient, and industrious.

Not parallel:

Knowing how to win is important, but it is even more important to know how to lose.

Parallel:

Knowing how to win is important, but knowing how to lose is even more important.

Not parallel:

We can go out to eat, or ordering a pizza would do as well.

Parallel:

We can go out to eat, or we can order a pizza.

Not parallel:

He has plundered our seas, ravaged our coasts, and was burning our towns.

Parallel:

He has plundered our seas, ravaged our coasts, and burned our towns.

Not parallel:

The only good is knowledge, and evil is the only ignorant thing.

Parallel:

The only good is knowledge, and the only evil is ignorance.

Not parallel:

Cursed be the social wants that sin against the strength of youth!

Cursed be the social ties that warp us from the living truth!

Cursed be the sickly forms that err from honest nature's rule!

The gold that gilds the straighten'd forehead of the fool is also cursed.

Parallel:

Cursed be the social wants that sin against the strength of youth!

Cursed be the social ties that warp us from the living truth!

Cursed be the sickly forms that err from honest nature's rule!

Cursed be the gold that gilds the straighten'd forehead of the fool.

PARALLEL ITEMS IN SERIES

Items in a series have greater impact when arranged in parallel form. The items can be words, phrases, or clauses:

Passions, prejudices, fears, and neuroses spring from ignorance, and take the form of myth and illusions.　　——Sir Isaiah Berlin

When any of the four pillars of the government, religion, justice, counsel, and treasure, are mainly shaken or weakened, men have need to pray for fair weather.
　　　　　　　　　　——Francis Bacon

In the opening of *A Tale of Two Cities*, Charles Dickens arranged paired items in a series for a powerful effect:

It was the best of times, it was the worst of times,
it was the age of wisdom, it was the age of foolishness,
it was the epoch of belief, it was the epoch of incredulity,
it was the season of Light, it was the season of Darkness,
it was the spring of hope, it was the winter of despair . . .

PARALLEL OUTLINES AND LISTS

Arranging outlined ideas and lists in parallel structure helps solidify logic. Maintaining one format (for example, complete sentences, clauses, or phrases) throughout serves to order ideas, as the following sentence outline shows:

I. Cigarette smoke harms the health of the general public.
   A. Cigarette smoke may lead to serious diseases in nonsmokers.
      1. It leads to lung disease.
         a. It causes emphysema.
         b. It causes cancer.
      2. It leads to circulatory disease.
         a. It causes strokes.
         b. It causes heart disease.
   B. Cigarette smoke worsens less serious health conditions in nonsmokers.
      1. It aggravates allergies.
      2. It intensifies pulmonary infections.

Usage

COMMON ERRORS

Language changes constantly. This glossary provides information about contemporary English usage, focusing on key errors made by native speakers. It will show you how certain words and phrases are used and why certain usage is unacceptable.

"Informal" indicates that a word or phrase is often used in everyday speech but should generally be avoided in formal discourse. "Nonstandard" means that the word or phrase is not suitable for everyday speech and writing in standard American English and should never be used in formal discourse.

a/an In both spoken and written English, *an* is used before words beginning with a vowel sound: **He carried an umbrella. The Nobel prize is an** honor, and when the consonants *f, h, l, m, n, r, s,* and *x* are pronounced by name: **The renovations created an L-shaped room. Miles received an F in physics.** Use *a* before words beginning with a consonant sound: **What a fish! I bought a computer,** and words that start with vowels but are pronounced as consonants: **A union can be dissolved. They live in a one-room apartment.** Also use *a* with words that start with consonant letters not listed above and with the vowel *u*: **She earned a C in French. He made a U-turn.**

For words that begin with *h*, if the initial *h* is not pronounced, the word is preceded by *an:* It will take an hour. Adjectives such as *historic, historical, heroic,* and *habitual* are commonly preceded by *an*, especially in British English, but the use of *a* is common in both writing and speech: She read a historical novel. When the *h* is strongly pronounced, as in a stressed first syllable, the word is preceded by *a*: I bought a history of Long Island

above *Above* can be used as an adjective The **above** entry is incomplete, or as a noun: First, please read the **above**, in referring to what has been previously mentioned in a passage. Both uses are standard in formal writing.

agree to/agree with *Agree to* means "to consent to, to accept" (usually a plan or idea). *Agree with* means "to be in accord with" (usually a person or group): I can't believe they will **agree to** the proposed merger when they don't **agree with** each other on anything.

ain't The term is nonstandard for *am not, isn't,* or *aren't*. It is used informally for humorous effect or to evoke dialectal speech, usually in dialogue.

all right/alright *All right* is always written as two words; *alright* is a misspelling: Betsy said that it was **all right** to use her car that afternoon.

almost/most *Almost,* an adverb, means "nearly"; *most,* an adjective, means "the greatest part of" something. *Most* is not synonymous with *almost,* as the following example shows: **During our vacation we shop at that store almost every day and buy most of the available snack foods.**

In informal speech, *most* (as a shortened form of *almost*) is used as an adverb. It occurs before such pronouns as *all, anybody, anyone, everybody,* and *everyone;* the adjectives *all, any,* and *every;* and the adverbs *anywhere* and *everywhere.* For example: **Most everyone around here is related.** The use of *most* as an adverb is nonstandard and is uncommon in formal writing except when used to represent speech.

A.M., P.M. These abbreviations for time are most frequently restricted to use with figures: **The ceremony begins at 10:00 A.M.** (not "ten thirty A.M.")

among/between *Among* is used to indicate relationships involving more than two people or things, while *between* is used to show relationships involving two people or things, or to compare one thing to a group to which it belongs: **The three quarreled among themselves because she had to choose between two of them.** *Between* is also used to express relationships of persons or things considered individually, no matter how many:

Between holding public office, teaching, and raising a family, she has little free time.

and etc. Since *etc.* means "and all the rest," *and etc.* is redundant; the *and* is not needed. Some writers prefer to use *and so forth* or *and the like* as a substitute for the abbreviation.

and/or The combination *and/or* is used mainly in legal and business writing. Its use should be avoided in general writing, as in: **He spends his weekends watching television and/or snacking.** In such writing, either one or the other word is sufficient. If you mean "either," use *or*; if you mean "both," use *and*. To make a greater distinction, revise the phrasing: **He spends his weekends watching television, snacking, or both.**

and which/and who *And* is unnecessary when *which* or *who* is used to open a relative clause. Use *and which* or *and who* only to open a second clause starting with the same relative pronoun: **Elizabeth is my neighbor who goes shopping every morning and who calls me every afternoon to tell me about the sales.**

a number/the number As a subject, *a number* is most often plural and *the number* is singular. **A number of choices are available. The number of choices is limited.** As with many agreement questions, this guideline is followed more often in formal discourse than in speech and informal writing.

anyplace *Anyplace* is an informal expression for *anywhere*. It occurs in speech and informal writing but is best avoided in formal prose.

anyways/anyway; anywheres/anywhere *Anyways* is nonstandard for *anyway*; *anywheres* is nonstandard for *anywhere*.

as Do not use *as* in place of *whether*: **We're not sure whether (not *as*) you should do that.** Also avoid using *as* as a substitute for *because, since, while, whether,* or *who,* where its use may create confusion. In the following sentence, for example, *as* may mean "while" or "because": **As they were driving to California they decided to see the Grand Canyon.**

as/because/since While all three words can function as subordinating conjunctions, they convey slightly different shades of meaning. *As* establishes a time relationship and can be used interchangeably with *when* or *while*. *Because* and *since*, in contrast, describe causes and effects: **As we brought out the food, it began to drizzle. Because (since) Nancy goes skiing infrequently, she prefers to rent skis.**

as/like When *as* functions as a preposition, the distinction between *as* and *like* depends on meaning: *As* suggests that the subject is equivalent to the description: **He was employed as a teacher.** *Like,* in contrast, suggests similarity but not equivalence: **Speakers like her excel in front of large groups.**

at Avoid using *at* with *where* in a question: **Where are you seeing her (not *at*)?** Whether used as an adverb or as a preposition, *where* contains the preposition *at* in its definition.

at this point in time Although the phrase *at this point in time* is widely used (especially in politics), many people consider it verbose and stuffy. Instead, use *now* or *at this time*: **We are not ready to discuss the new budget now.**

awful/awfully Avoid using *awful* or *awfully* to mean "very" in formal discourse: **We had an awfully busy day at the amusement park.** Although the use of *awful* to mean "terrible" (rather than "inspiring awe") has permeated all levels of writing and speech, consider using in its place a word that more closely matches your intended meaning: **We had an unpleasant (not *awful*) time because the park was hot, noisy, and crowded.**

awhile/a while *Awhile* is an adverb and is always spelled as one word: **We visited awhile.** *A while* is a noun phrase (an article and a noun) and is used after a preposition: **We rested for a while.**

backward/backwards In formal discourse, *backward* is preferred: **This stroke is easier if you use a backward motion (adjec-**

tive). Counting **backward** from 100 can be an effective way to induce sleep (adverb).

bad/badly *Bad*, an adjective, is used to describe a noun or pronoun. *Badly*, an adverb, is used to describe a verb, adjective, or another adverb. Thus: She felt **bad** because her broken leg throbbed **badly**.

because/due to the fact that/since *Because* or *since* are preferred over the wordy phrase *due to the fact that*: He wrote the report longhand **because** (not *due to the fact that*) his computer was broken.

being as/being that Avoid both *being as* and *being that* in formal writing. Instead, use *since* or *because*. For example: **Since** you asked, I'll be glad to help.

better/had better The verb *had* is necessary in the phrase *had better* and should be retained in formal speech. She **had better** return the lawn mower today.

between you and I Although this phrase is heard occasionally in the speech of even educated people, it is incorrect. Pronouns that function as objects of prepositions should be in the objective case. Please keep this **between you and me**. I would appreciate it if you could keep this **between her and them**.

bi- Many words that refer to periods of time through the prefix *bi-* are potentially confusing. Ambiguity is avoided by using the prefix *semi-*, meaning "twice each" (**semi-weekly, semimonthly, semiannual**) or by using the appropriate phrases (**twice a week, twice each month, every two months; every two years**).

borrow off/borrow from *Borrow off*, considered informal, should not be used in formal speech and writing; *borrow from* is the preferred expression.

bottom line This overworked term is frequently used as a synonym for *outcome* or *the final result*: **The bottom line is that we have to reduce inventory to maintain profits.** Careful writers and speakers avoid it for less shopworn descriptions.

bunch Use the noun *bunch* in formal writing only to refer to clusters of things grouped together, such as grapes or bananas: **That bunch of grapes looks better than the other one.** In formal writing, use *group* or *crowd* to refer to gatherings of people; *bunch* is used to refer to groups of people or items only in speech and informal writing.

burst, bursted/bust, busted *Burst* is a verb meaning "to come apart suddenly." The word *bursted* is not acceptable in either speech or writing. The verb *bust* and adjective *busted* are both informal or slang terms; as such, they should not be used in formal writing.

but however/but yet There is no reason to combine *but* with another conjunction:

She said she was leaving, **yet** (not *but yet*) she poured another cup of coffee.

but that/but what As with the previous example, there is no reason to add the word *but* to either *that* or *what*: We don't doubt **that** (not *but that*) you will win this hand.

calculate/figure/reckon None of these words is an acceptable substitute for *expect* or *imagine* in formal writing, although they are all used in speech and informal prose.

can/may Traditionally, *may* is used in formal writing to convey permission; *can* to convey ability or capacity. In speech, however, the terms are used interchangeably to mean permission: **Can (May) I borrow your hedge clippers?** *Can* and *may* are frequently, but not always, interchangeable when used to mean possibility: **A blizzard can (or may) occur any time during February.** In negative constructions, *can't* is more common than *mayn't*, the latter being extremely rare and stilted: **You can't eat that taco in the den.**

cannot/can not *Cannot* is occasionally spelled *can not*. The one-word spelling is by far the more common. The contraction *can't* is used mainly in speech and informal writing.

can't help but *Can't help but*, as in: **You can't help but like her,** is a double negative. This idiom can be replaced by the informal *can't help* or the formal *cannot but* where each is appropriate: **She can't help** wishing that it was spring. **I cannot but** wish things had turned out differently. While *can't help but* is common in all types of speech, you should avoid using it in formal writing.

cause of . . . on account of/due to The phrases *on account of* and *due to* are unnecessary with *cause of*: One **cause of** physical and psychological problems is **due to** too much stress. Omit the phrases or revise the entire sentence. Change the sentence to: Too much stress **causes** physical and psychological problems.

center around/center on Although both phrases are often criticized for being illogical, they have been used in writing for more than a hundred years to express the notion of collecting or gathering as if around a center point. The phrase *revolve around* is often suggested as an alternative, and the prepositions *at*, *in*, and *on* are considered acceptable with *center* in the following sense: Their problems **centered on** their lack of expertise.

chair/chairperson *Chairperson* is used widely in academic and governmental circles as an alternative to *chairman* or *chairwoman*. While some reject the term *chairperson* as clumsy and unnecessary and use the term *chair* for any presiding officer, regardless of sex, *chairperson* is still standard in all types of writing and speech.

choose/chose *Choose* is a verb that means "to select one thing in preference to another": **Why choose tomatoes when they are out of season?** *Chose* is the past tense of *to choose*: **I chose tomatoes over cucumbers at the salad bar.**

conformity to/conformity with Although the word *conformity* can be followed by either *to* or *with*, *conformity to* is generally used when the idea of obedience is implied: **The new commissioner issued a demand for conformity to health regulations.** *Conformity with* is used to imply agreement or correspondence: **This is an idea in conformity with previous planning.**

consensus/consensus of The expression *consensus of* (consensus of opinion) is considered redundant, and the preferred usage is the single noun *consensus*, meaning "general agreement or concord": **Since the consensus was overwhelming, the city planners moved ahead with the proposal.** The phrase *general consensus* is also considered redundant. Increasingly, the word *consensus* is widely used attributively, as in the phrase *consensus politics*.

contact The word is both a verb and a noun. As a verb, it is frequently used unprecisely to mean "to communicate" when a more exact word (telephone, write to, consult) would better communicate the idea. *Contact* as a noun meaning "a person through whom one can obtain information" is now standard usage: **He is my contact in the state department.**

couple/couple of Both phrases are informally used to mean "two" or "several": **I need a couple more cans of paint. I took a couple of aspirins for my headache.** The expression *a couple of* is used in standard English, especially in referring to distance, money, or time: **He is a couple of feet away. I have a couple of thousand dollars in the bank. The store will open in a couple of weeks.** *Couple* may be treated as either a singular or plural noun.

criteria/criterion *Criteria* is the plural of *criterion* (a standard for judgment). For example: **Of all their criteria for evaluating job performance, customer satisfaction was the most important criterion.**

data/datum *Data* is the plural of *datum* (fact). Although *data* is often used as a singular, it should still be treated as plural in formal speech and writing: **The data pertain** (not *pertains*) **to the first half of the experiment.** To avoid awkward constructions, most writers prefer to use a more commonplace term such as *fact* or *figure* in place of *datum*.

decimate The word *decimate* comes from a Latin term that meant "to select by lot and kill one person in ten of (a rebellious military unit)." The usual use of the word in English is "to destroy a large amount or proportion of": **Disease decimated the**

population. Some people claim that *decimate* should only be used to mean "to destroy a tenth of," but in fact there is nothing wrong with the sense "to destroy a large amount or proportion of."

differ from/differ with *Differ from* means "to be unlike"; *differ with* means "to disagree with": The sisters **differ from** each other in appearance. We **differ with** you on this matter.

different from/different than Although *different from* is the preferred usage (His attitude is **different from** mine), *different than* is widely accepted when a clause follows, especially when the word *from* would create an awkward sentence. Example: The stream followed a **different** course **than** the map showed.

don't/does not *Don't* is the contraction for *do not*, not for *does not*, as in I **don't** care, she **doesn't** (not *don't*) care. The use of *don't* as a contraction for *does not* is nonstandard.

done Using *done* as an adjective to mean "through, finished" is standard. Originally, *done* was used attributively The pact between them was a **done** thing, but it has become more common as a complement: Are your pictures **done** yet? When we were **done** with the power saw, we removed the blade.

double negatives Double negatives are universally considered unacceptable: He

didn't have nothing to do, for example. In standard speech and writing, *anything* would be used in place of *nothing*. There are certain uses of double negation, to express an affirmative, that are considered standard, however: **We cannot sit here and do nothing,** meaning "we must do something."

doubt that/doubt whether/doubt if *Doubt that* is used to express conviction **I doubt that they intended to hurt your feelings;** *doubt whether* and *doubt if* are used to indicate uncertainty: **I doubt whether (or if) anyone really listened to the speaker.**

due to In formal discourse, *due to* is acceptable only after a form of the verb *to be*: **Her aching back was due to poor posture.** *Due to* is not acceptable as a preposition meaning *because of* or *owing to*: **Because of** (not *due to*) poor weather, the bus was late.

each When *each* is used as a pronoun, it takes a singular verb: **Each was born in Europe,** although plurals are increasingly used in formal speech and writing in an attempt to avoid using *he* or *his* for sentences that include females or do not specify sex: **Each of them had their (rather than** *his*) **own agenda.** More and more, the same pattern of pronoun agreement is being used with the singular pronouns *anybody, anyone, everybody, everyone, no one, somebody,* and *someone.* When the pronoun *each* is followed by an *of*-phrase containing a plural noun or pronoun, usage guides suggest that the verb be singular, but the plural is used often even in formal writing: Each of the children **has (or have)** had a school physical.

When the adjective *each* follows a plural subject, the verb agrees with the subject: The rooms each **have** separate thermostats.

each and every Use *each* or *every* in place of the phrase *each and every*, generally considered wordy: **Each** of us enjoyed the concert. **Every** one of us stayed until the end of the performance.

each other/one another *Each other* is traditionally used to indicate two members; *one another* for three or more: The two children trade lunches with **each other**. The guests greeted **one another** fondly. In standard practice, though, these distinctions are not observed in either speech or writing.

enormity The word *enormity* means "outrageousness; atrociousness; monstrousness": the **enormity** of his crime. It is often used to mean "great size; enormousness": The **enormity** of the task overwhelmed her. Though this second use is common, many people consider it to be an error.

enthused/enthusiastic The word *enthused* is used informally to mean "showing enthusiasm." For formal writing and speech, use the adjective *enthusiastic*: **The team was enthusiastic** about the quarterback's winning play.

-ess/-or/-er The suffix *-ess* has often been used to denote feminine nouns. While many such words are still in use, English is moving increasingly toward nouns that do not denote sex differences. The most widely observed guideline today is that if the sex of the performer is not relevant to the performance of the task or function, the neutral ending *-or* or *-er* should be used in place of *-ess*. Thus, words such as *ambassadress*, *ancestress*, *authoress*, *poetess*, *proprietress*, and *sculptress* are no longer used, and the airlines, for example, have replaced both *steward* and *stewardess* with *flight attendant*.

et al. *Et al.*, the Latin abbreviation for *and other people*, is fully standard for use in a citation to refer to works with more than three authors: **Harris et al.**

etc. Since *etc.* (et cetera) is the Latin abbreviation for *and other things*, it should not be used to refer to people. In general, it should be avoided in formal writing as imprecise. In its place, provide the entire list of items or use *and so on*.

-ette English nouns whose *-ette* ending signifies a feminine role or identity are passing out of usage. *Suffragette* and *usherette*, for example, have been replaced by *suffragist* and *usher*, respectively.

everywheres/everywhere *Everywheres* is a nonstandard term for *everywhere* and should be avoided in speech and writing.

except for the fact that/except that Use *except that* in place of the verbose phrase *except for the fact that*: **Except that** (not *except for the fact that*) the button is missing, this is a lovely skirt.

fewer/less Traditionally, *fewer*, a plural noun, has most often been used to refer to individual units that can be counted: There are **fewer** buttons on this shirt. No **fewer** than forty of the fifty voters supported the measure. *Less*, a singular noun, is used to refer to uncountable quantities: She eats **less** every day. I have **less** patience than I used to.

Standard English does not usually reflect these distinctions, however. When followed by *than*, *less* is used as often as *fewer* to indicate plural countable nouns. There were no **less than** eight million people. No **less than** forty of the fifty voters supported the measure.

figuratively/literally *Figuratively* means "involving a figure of speech": The poet Robert Frost once **figuratively** described writing poetry without regular meter and rhyme as playing tennis with the net down. *Literally* means: "In the literal or strict sense": What does the word mean **literally**?

Literally is commonly used as an intensifier meaning "in effect, virtually": The state representative was **literally** buried alive in the caucus. This usage is often criticized and should be avoided in formal discourse.

fix The verb *fix*, meaning "to repair," is fully accepted in all areas of speech and writing. The noun *fix*, meaning "repair" or "adjustment," is used informally.

fixing to/intend to Use *intend to* in place of the informal or dialectal term *fixing to*: The community **intends to** (not *is fixing to*) raise money to help the victims of the recent fire.

flunk/fail Use the standard term *fail* in speech and writing; *flunk* is an informal substitute.

former/latter *Former* is used to refer to the first of two items; *latter*, the second: We enjoy both gardening and painting, the **former** during the summer and the **latter** during the winter. When dealing with three or more items, use *first* and *last* rather than *former* and *latter*: We enjoy gardening, painting, and skiing, but the **last** is very costly.

fortuitous *Fortuitous* means "happening accidentally": A **fortuitous** meeting with a former acquaintance led to a change in plans. It is also used sometimes as a synonym for *lucky* or *fortunate*.

from whence Although the phrase *from whence* is sometimes criticized on the grounds that *from* is redundant because it is included in the meaning of *whence*, the idiom is nonetheless standard in both speech and writing: **She finally moved to Kansas, from whence she began to build a new life.**

fulsome Originally, *fulsome* meant "abundant," but for hundreds of years the word has been used to mean "offensive, disgusting, or excessively lavish." While the word still maintains the connotations of "excessive" or "offensive," it has also come to be used in the original sense as well: **Compare the severe furniture of the living room to the fulsome decorations in the den.**

fun *Fun* should not be used as an adjective in formal writing. Instead, substitute a word such as *happy*, *pleasant*, or *entertaining*: **They had a pleasant (not *fun*) afternoon at the park.**

gentlemān Once used only to refer to men of high social rank, the term *gentleman* now also specifies a man of courtesy and consideration: **He behaves like a gentleman.** It is also used as a term of polite reference and address in the singular and plural: **This gentleman is waiting to be served. Are we ready to begin, gentlemen?**

get The verb *get* is used in many slang and informal phrases as a substitute for forms of *to be*. For example: **They won't get accepted with that attitude.** In American English, an alternative past participle is *gotten,* especially in the sense of *received* and *acquired*: I **have gotten** (or **got**) all I ever wanted.

Both *have* and *has got* (meaning *must*) are occasionally criticized as being redundant, but are nonetheless fully standard in all varieties of speech and writing: You **have got** to carry your driver's license at all times.

good/well *Good,* an adjective, should be used to describe someone or something: Joe is a **good** student. *Well,* when used as an adverb, should describe an action: She and Laura play **well** together on the swing set. *Well,* when used as an adjective after *look, feel,* or other linking verbs, often refers to good health: You're looking **well.**

good and/very Avoid using *good and* as a substitute for *very*: I was **very** (not *good and*) hungry.

graduate The passive form, once considered the only correct usage, is seldom used today: I was **graduated** from the Merchant Marine Academy last May. Although some critics condemn the use of *graduate* as a verb meaning "to receive a degree or diploma (from)," its use is common in both speech and writing: She **graduated** from high school in Cleveland.

great The word *great* has been overused in informal writing and speech as a synonym for *enthusiastic, good,* or *clever*: She was really **great** at making people feel at home.

had drank/had drunk According to some authorities, *had drank* is acceptable usage: I **had drank** a gallon of milk. *Had drunk*, though, is fully standard and the preferred usage.

had ought/ought *Had ought* is considered wordy; the preferred usage is *ought*: She **ought** (not *had ought*) to heed her mother's advice.

half/a half a/a half Use either *half* or *a half*; *a half a* is wordy: Please give me **a half** (not *a half a*) piece. I'd like **half** that slice, please.

hanged/hung Although both words are past-tense forms of *to hang*, *hanged* is used to refer to executions: Billy Budd was **hanged**, and *hung* is used for all other meanings: The stockings were **hung** by the chimney with care.

has/have; has got/have got The word *got* is unnecessary; simply use *has* or *have*: Jessica **has** a mild case of chicken pox.

have/of Use *have* rather than *of* after helping verbs like *could*, *should*, *would*, *may*, and *might*: They should **have** (not *of*) let me know of their decision earlier.

he, she; he/she; s/he The pronouns *he* and *she* refer to male and female antecedents, respectively. Traditionally, when an antecedent in singular form could be either female or male, *he* was always used to refer to either sex: A child is often apprehensive when **he** first begins school. Today, however, various approaches have been developed to avoid the all-purpose *he*. Many people find the construction *he/she* (*he or she*) awkward: A child is often apprehensive when **he/she** first begins school. The blended form *s/he* has not been widely adopted, probably because of confusion over pronunciation. Most people now favor either rephrasing the sentence entirely to omit the pronoun or reconstructing the sentence in the third-person plural: Children are often apprehensive when **they** first begin school.

hopefully *Hopefully* originally meant "in a hopeful manner": The beggar looked up **hopefully**. It is now usually used to mean "it is to be hoped; I hope; let us hope": **Hopefully, we'll get there on time.** Although this sense is common and standard, many people consider it incorrect.

how come/why *How come* is used informally in speech. In formal speech and writing, use *why*.

if/whether Use *whether* rather than *if* to begin a subordinate clause when the clause states a choice: I don't know **whether** (not *if*) I should stay until the end or leave right after the opening ceremony.

impact Both the noun and verb *impact* are used to indicate forceful contact: I cannot overstate the **impact** of the new policy on productivity. Some speakers and writers avoid using *impact* as a verb to mean "to have an effect," as in: Our work here **impacts** on every division in the firm.

in Several phrases beginning with *in* are verbose and should be avoided in formal writing. Refer to the following table.

Replace the phrase	With
in this day and age	now
in spite of the fact that	although or even though
in the neighborhood of	approximately or about
in the event that	if

The following phrases can be omitted entirely:

in a very real sense
in number
in nature
in reality
in terms of
and in the case of

in/into *In* is used to indicate condition or location, "positioned within": She was **in** labor. The raccoon was **in** the woodpile. *Into*, in contrast, indicates movement or a change in condition "from the outside to the inside": The raccoon went **into** the shed. He went **into** cardiac arrest. *Into* is also used as a slang expression for *involved with* or *interested in*: **They are really** **into** **health foods.**

inferior than *Inferior to* and *worse than* are the generally preferred forms: **This wine is** **inferior to** (not *inferior than*) **the bur-gundy we had last night.**

in regards to/with regards to Both terms are considered nonstandard terms for *regarding, in regard to, with regard to,* and *as regards*: **As regards** (not *in regards to*) **your request of April 1, we have traced your shipment and it will be delivered tomorrow.**

inside/outside; inside of/outside of When the words *inside* and *outside* are used as prepositions, the word *of* is not included: **Stay** **inside** **the house. The authorization is** **outside** **my department.** *Inside of* is used informally to refer to time: **I'll be there** **inside of** **an hour,** but in formal speech or writing *within* is the preferred usage: **The dump was cleaned up** **within** **a month.**

insignia *Insignia* was originally the plural of the Latin word *insigne*. The plural term *insignias* has been standard usage since the eighteenth century.

irregardless/regardless *Regardless* is the standard term; avoid *irregardless* in both speech and writing.

is when/is where Both phrases are non-standard and are to be avoided in speech and writing.

its/it's/its' *Its* is the possessive form of *it*: **The shrub is losing its blossoms.** *It's* is the contraction for *it is*: **It's a nice day.** The two are often confused because possessives are most frequently formed with -*'s*. *Its'* is nonstandard usage.

It's me/It's I The traditional rule is that personal pronouns after the verb *to be* take the nominative case (*I, she, he, we, they*). Today, however, such usage as *it's me, that's him, it must be them* is almost universal in informal speech. The objective forms have also replaced the nominative forms in informal speech in such constructions as *me neither* and *who, them?* In formal discourse, however, the nominative forms are still used: **it's I, that is he.**

-ize/-wise Use the suffix -*ize* to change a noun or adjective into a verb: **categorize.** Use the suffix -*wise* to change a noun or adjective into an adverb: **otherwise.**

kind of/sort of/type of Avoid using either *kind of*, *sort of*, or *type of* as synonyms for *somewhat* in formal speech and writing. Instead, use *rather*: **She was rather** (not *kind of*) **slender.** It is acceptable to use the three terms only when the word *kind, sort,* or *type* is stressed: **This kind of cheese is hard to digest.** Do not add *a*: **I don't know what kind of** (not *kind of a*) **cheese that is.** When the word *kind, sort,* or *type* is not stressed, omit the phrase entirely: **That's an unusual** (not *unusual* *kind of*) car. She's a **pleasant** (not *pleasant sort of a*) person.

let's *Let's* is often used as a word in its own right rather than as the contraction of *let us*. As such, it is often used in informal speech and writing with redundant or appositional pronouns: **Let's us take in a movie. Let's you and me go for a walk.** Usage guides suggest avoiding *let's us* in formal speech and writing, although both *let's you and me* and *let's you and I* occur in the everyday speech of educated speakers. While the former conforms to the traditional rules of grammar, the latter occurs more frequently.

like/such as Use *like* to compare an example to the thing mentioned and *such as* to show that the example is representative of the thing mentioned: **Molly wants to be a famous clothing designer like John Weitz, Liz Claiborne, and Yves St. Laurent. Molly has samples of many fine articles such as evening dresses, suits, and jackets.**

Many writers favor not separating *such* and *as* with an intervening word: **samples of many fine articles such as**, rather than: **samples of such fine articles as**.

lots/lots of Both terms are used in informal speech and writing as a substitute for *a great many*, *very many*, or *much*.

man The use of the term *man* as a synonym for *human being*, both by itself and in compounds (*mankind*), is declining. Terms such as *human being(s)*, *human race*, *humankind*, *humanity*, *people*, and, when necessary, *men and women* or *women and men* are widely accepted in formal usage.

-man/-person The use of the term *-man* as the last element in compound words referring to a person of either sex who performs some function (*anchorman*, *chairman*, *spokesman*) has declined in recent years. Now such compound words are widely used only if the word refers to a male. The sex-neutral word *person* is otherwise substituted for *man* (*anchorperson*, *chairperson*, *spokesperson*). In other instances, a form without a suffix (*anchor*, *chair*), or a word that does not denote gender (*speaker*), is used.

The compound words *freshman*, *lowerclassmen*, *underclassmen* are still generally used in schools, and *freshman* is used in the U.S. Congress as well. These terms are applied to members of both sexes. As a modifier, *freshman* is used with both singular and plural nouns: *freshman athlete*, *freshman legislators*. See also **chair/chairperson**.

me and *Me and* is considered nonstandard usage when part of a compound subject: **Donna and I** (not *Me and Donna*) decided to fly to Boston.

media *Media*, the plural of medium, is used with a plural verb: Increasingly, the radio and television **media seem** to be stressing sensational news.

mighty *Mighty* is used informally for *very* or *extremely*: He is a **mighty** big fighter.

more important/more importantly Both phrases are acceptable in standard English: My donations of clothing were tax deduct-ible; **more important(ly)**, the clothes were given to homeless people.

Ms. (or Ms) The title *Ms.* is widely used in business and professional circles as an alternative to *Mrs.* and *Miss*, both of which reveal a woman's marital status. Some women prefer *Mrs.*, where appropriate, or the traditional *Miss*, which is still fully standard for an unmarried woman or a woman whose marital status is unknown. Since *Ms.* is not an abbreviation, some sources spell it without a period, others use a period to parallel *Mr.* It is correctly used before a woman's name but not before her husband's name: **Ms. Elizabeth Poff** or **Ms. Poff** (not *Ms. Ken Poff*).

much/many Use *many* rather than *much* to modify plural nouns: They had **many** (not *much*) dogs. There were too **many** (not *much*) facts to absorb.

Muslim/Moslem *Muslim* is now the preferred form for an adherent of Islam, though *Moslem*, the traditional form, is still in use.

mutual One current meaning of *mutual* is "reciprocal": Employers and employees sometimes suffer from a **mutual** misunderstanding. Mutual can also mean "held in common, shared": Their **mutual** goal is clearly understood.

myself; herself; himself; yourself The *-self* pronouns are intensive or reflexive, intensifying or referring to an antecedent: **Kerri herself said so. Mike and I did it ourselves.** Questions are raised when the *-self* forms are used instead of personal pronouns (I, me, etc.) as subjects, objects, or complements. This use of the *-self* forms is especially common in informal speech and writing: **Many came to welcome my wife and myself back from China.** All these forms are also used, alone or with other nouns or pronouns, after *as*, *than*, or *but* in all varieties of speech and writing: **Letters have arrived for everyone but the counselors and yourselves.** Although there is ample precedent in both British and American usage for the expanded uses of the *-self* constructions, the *-self* pronouns should be used in formal speech and writing only with the nouns and pronouns to which they refer: **No one except me** (not *myself*) **saw the movie.**

nauseous/nauseated *Nauseated* is generally preferred in formal writing over *nauseous*: **The wild ride on the roller coaster made Meghan feel nauseated.**

neither . . . nor When used as a correlative, *neither* is almost always followed by

nor: **neither** Heather **nor** her father . . .
The subjects connected by *neither . . . nor*
take a singular verb when both subjects
are singular: **Neither** Heather **nor** her
father **is going** to watch the program,
and a plural verb when both are plural:
Neither the rabbits **nor** the sheep **have
been** fed yet today. When a singular and
a plural subject are joined by these correl-
atives, the verb should agree with the
nearer noun or pronoun: **Neither** the
mayor **nor** the council members **have**
yielded. **Neither** the council members
nor the mayor **has** yielded.

nohow The word *nohow*, nonstandard
usage for *in no way* or *in any way*, should
be avoided in speech and writing.

none *None* can be treated as either singular
or plural depending on its meaning in a
sentence. When the sense is "not any persons or things," the plural is more common: **The rescue party searched for survivors, but none were** found. When *none*
is clearly intended to mean "not one" or
"not any," it is followed by a singular verb:
**Of all the ailments I have diagnosed dur-
ing my career, none has been** stranger
than yours.

no . . . nor/no . . . or Use *no . . . or* in compound phrases: We had **no** milk **or** eggs
in the house.

nothing like, nowhere near Both phrases
are used in informal speech and writing,

but they should be avoided in formal discourse. Instead, use *not nearly*: **The congealed pudding found in the back of the refrigerator is not nearly as old as the stale bread on the second shelf.**

nowheres/nowhere The word *nowheres*, nonstandard usage for *nowhere*, should be avoided in speech and writing.

of Avoid using *of* with descriptive adjectives after the adverbs *how* or *too* in formal speech and writing. This usage is largely restricted to informal discourse: **How long of a ride will it be? It's too cold of a day for swimming.**

off of/off *Off of* is redundant and awkward; use *off*: **The cat jumped off the sofa.**

OK/O.K./okay All three spellings are considered acceptable, but the phrases are generally reserved for informal speech and writing.

on account of/because of Since it is less wordy, *because of* is the preferred phrase: **Because of her headache, they decided to go straight home.**

on the one hand/on the other hand These two transitions should be used together: **On the one hand, we hoped for fair weather. On the other hand, we knew the rain was needed for the crops.** This usage, though, can be wordy. Effective substitutes include *in contrast*, *but*, *however*, and *yet*: **We hoped for fair weather, yet we knew the rain was needed for the crops.**

only The placement of *only* as a modifier is more a matter of style and clarity than of grammatical rule. In strict formal usage, *only* should be placed as close as possible before the word it modifies. In the following sentence, for example, the placement of the word *only* suggests that no one but the children was examined: **The doctor examined only the children.** In the next sentence, the placement of *only* says that no one but the doctor did the examining: **Only the doctor examined the children.** Nonetheless, in all types of speech and writing, people often place *only* before the verb regardless of what it modifies. In spoken discourse, speakers may convey their intended meaning by stressing the word or construction to which *only* applies.

owing to the fact that *Because* is generally accepted as a less wordy substitute for *owing to the fact that*.

pair/pairs When modified by a number, the plural of *pair* is commonly *pairs*, especially when referring to persons: **The three pairs of costumed children led off the Halloween parade.** The plural *pair* is used mainly in reference to inanimate objects or nonhumans: **There are four pair (or pairs) of shoelaces. We have two pair (or pairs) of rabbits.**

people/persons In formal usage, *people* is most often used to refer to a general group, emphasizing anonymity: **We the people** of the United States . . . Use *persons* to indicate any unnamed individuals within the group: **Will the persons who left their folders on the table please pick them up at their earliest convenience?** Except when individuals are being emphasized, *people* is generally used rather than *persons*.

per; a/an *Per*, meaning "for each," occurs mainly in technical or statistical contexts: **This new engine averages fifty miles per hour. Americans eat fifty pounds of chicken per person per year.** It is also frequently used in sports commentary: **He scored an average of two runs per game.** *A* or *an* is often considered more suitable in nontechnical use: **The silk costs twenty dollars a yard. How many miles an hour can you walk?**

percent/per cent *Percent* was originally spelled *per cent*, an abbreviation of the Latin *per centum*. It almost always follows a number: **I made 12 percent interest by investing my money in that new account.** In formal writing, use the word rather than the symbol (%). The use of the two-word form *per cent* is diminishing.

phenomena Like words such as *criteria* and *media*, *phenomena* is a plural form (of *phenomenon*), meaning "observable facts, occurrences, or circumstances": **The offi-**

cial explained that the disturbing **phe-nomena** we had seen for the past three evenings were nothing more than routine aircraft maneuvers.

plenty As a noun, *plenty* is acceptable in standard usage: I have **plenty** of money. In informal speech and writing, *plenty* is often a substitute for *very*: She was traveling **plenty** fast down the freeway.

plus *Plus* is a preposition meaning "in addition to": My salary **plus** overtime is enough to allow us a gracious lifestyle. Recently, *plus* has been used as a conjunctive adverb in informal speech and writing: It's safe, **plus** it's economical. Many people object to this use.

practically Use *practically* as a synonym for *in effect*, or *virtually*. It is also considered correct to use it in place of *nearly* in all varieties of speech and writing.

previous to/prior to *Before* is generally preferred in place of either expression: **Before** (not *previous to* or *prior to*) repairing the tire, you should check to see if there are any other leaks.

providing/provided Both forms can serve as subordinating conjunctions meaning "on the condition that": **Provided (Providing)** that we get the contract in time, we will be able to begin work by the first of the month. While some critics feel that *provided* is more acceptable in formal discourse, both are correct.

rarely ever/rarely/hardly The term *rarely ever* is used informally in speech and writing. For formal discourse, use either *rarely* or *hardly* in place of *rarely ever*: **She rarely calls her mother. She hardly calls her mother.**

real/really In formal usage, *real* (an adjective meaning "genuine") should not be used in place of *really* (an adverb meaning "actually"): **The platypus hardly looked real. How did it really happen?**

reason is because/reason is since Although both expressions are commonly used in informal speech and writing, formal usage requires a clause beginning with *that* after *reason is*: **The reason the pool is empty is that** (not *because* or *since*) **the town recently imposed a water restriction.** Another alternative is to recast the sentence: **The pool is empty because the town recently imposed a water restriction.**

regarding/in regard to/with regard to/ relating to/relative to/with respect to/respecting All the above expressions are formal substitutes for *about, concerning,* or *on*: **Janet spoke about** (not *regarding, relative to,* etc.) **the PTA's plans for the September fund drive.**

relate to The phrase *relate to* is used informally to mean "understand" or "respond in a sympathetic manner": **I can't relate**

to what you're talking about. It is rarely used in formal writing or speech.

repeat it/repeat it again *Repeat it* is the expression to use to indicate someone should say something for a second time: **I did not hear your name; please repeat it.** *Repeat it again* indicates the answer is to be said a third time. In the majority of instances, *repeat it* is the desired phrase; *again*, an unnecessary addition.

says/said Use *said* rather than *says* after a verb in the past tense: **At the public meeting, he stood up and said** (not *says*), "**The bond issue cannot pass.**"

seldom ever/seldom *Seldom* is the preferred form in formal discourse: **They seldom** (not *seldom ever*) **go to the beach.**

shall/will Today, *shall* is used for first-person questions requesting consent or opinion. **Shall we go for a drive? Shall I buy this dress or that?** *Shall* can also be used in the first person to create an elevated tone: **We shall call on you at six o'clock.** It is sometimes used with the second or third person to state a speaker's resolution: **You shall obey me.**

Traditionally, *will* was used for the second and third persons: **Will you attend the party? Will he and she go as well?** It is now widely used in speech and writing as the future-tense helping verb for all three persons: **I will drive, you will drive, they will drive.**

should/would Rules similar to those for choosing between *shall* and *will* have long been advanced for *should* and *would*. In current American usage, use of *would* far outweighs that of *should*. *Should* is chiefly used to state obligation: **I should repair the faucet. You should get the parts we need.** *Would*, in contrast, is used to express a hypothetical situation or a wish: **I would like to go. Would you?**

since *Since* is an adverb meaning "from then until now": **She was appointed in May and has been supervisor ever since.** It is also used as an adverb meaning "between a particular past time and the present; subsequently": **They had at first refused to cooperate, but have since agreed to volunteer.** As a preposition, since means "continuously from": **It has been rainy since June.** It is also used as a preposition meaning "between a past time or event and the present": **There have been many changes since the merger.** As a conjunction, *since* means "in the period following the time when": **He has called since he changed jobs.** *Since* is also used as a synonym for *because*: **Since you're here early, let's begin.**

situation The word *situation* is often added unnecessarily to a sentence: **The situation is that we must get the painting done by the weekend.** In such instances, consider revising the sentence to pare excess words: **We must get the painting done by the weekend.**

slow/slowly Today *slow* is used chiefly in spoken imperative constructions with short verbs that express motion, such as *drive, walk, swim,* and *run.* For example: **Drive slow. Don't walk so slow.** *Slow* is also combined with present participles to form adjectives: **He was slow-moving. It was a slow-burning fire.** *Slowly* is found commonly in formal writing and is used in both speech and writing before a verb: **He slowly walked through the hills,** as well as after a verb: **He walked slowly through the hills.**

so Many writers object to *so* being used as an intensifier, noting that in such usage it is often vague: **They were so happy.** *So* followed by *that* and a clause usually eliminates the vagueness: **They were so happy that they had been invited to the exclusive party.**

so/so that *So that,* rather than *so,* is most often used in formal writing to avoid the possibility of ambiguity: **He visited Aunt Lucia so that he could help her clean the basement.**

some *Some* is often used in informal speech and writing as an adjective meaning "exceptional, unusual" and as an adverb meaning "somewhat." In more formal instances, use *somewhat* in place of *some* as an adverb or a more precise word such as *remarkable* in place of *some* as an adjective: Those are **unusual** (not *some*) shoes. My sister and brother-in-law are going to have to rush **somewhat** (not *some*) to get here in time for dinner.

someplace/somewhere *Someplace* should be used only in informal writing and speech; use *somewhere* for formal discourse.

somewheres Somewheres is not accepted in formal writing or speech; use the standard *somewhere*: She would like to go **somewhere** (not *somewheres*) special to celebrate New Year's Eve.

split infinitive There is a longstanding convention that prohibits placing a word between *to* and the verb: **To understand fully another culture, you have to live among its people for many years.** This convention is based on an analogy with Latin, in which an infinitive is only one word and therefore cannot be divided. Criticism of the split infinitive was particularly strong when the modeling of English on Latin was especially popular, as it was in the nineteenth century. Today many people note that a split infinitive sometimes creates a less awkward sentence: **Many American companies expect to more than double their overseas investments in the next decade.**

suppose to/supposed to; use to/used to Both *suppose to* and *use to* are incorrect. The preferred usage is *supposed to* or *used to*: I was **supposed to** (not *suppose to*) get up early this morning to go hiking in the mountains. I **used to** (not *use to*) enjoy the seashore, but now I prefer the mountains.

sure/surely When used as an adverb meaning *surely*, *sure* is considered inappropriate for formal discourse. A qualifier like *certainly* should be used instead of *sure*: **My neighbors were certainly right about it.** It is widely used, however, in speech and informal writing: **They were sure right about that car.**

sure and/sure to; try and/try to *Sure to* and *try to* are the preferred forms for formal discourse: **Be sure to** (not *sure and*) **come home early tonight. Try to** (not *try and*) **avoid the traffic on the interstate.**

that The conjunction *that* is occasionally omitted, especially after verbs of thinking, saying, believing, and so forth: **She said (***that***) they would come by train.** The omission is most frequent in informal speech and writing, and almost always occurs when the dependent clause begins with a personal pronoun or a proper name.

that/which Traditionally, *that* is used to introduce a restrictive clause: **They should buy the cookies that the neighbor's child is selling.** *Which*, in contrast, is used to introduce nonrestrictive clauses: **The cookies, which are covered in chocolate, would make a nice evening snack.** This distinction is maintained far more often in formal writing than in everyday speech, where voice can often distinguish restrictive from nonrestrictive clauses.

that/which/who The relative pronoun *that* is used to refer to animals, things, and people. It can substitute in most cases for either *which* or *who(m)*: **The hitchhiker that (or whom) we picked up was a student.** In accepted usage, *who* is used only to refer to people. *Which* is used to refer to animals and inanimate objects: **The pen, which you bought, is out of ink. The doctor, who participates in our insurance plan, is very nice.**

them/those *Them* is nonstandard when used as an adjective: **I enjoyed those (not *them*) apples very much.**

they/their/them Although the word *they* is traditionally a third-person plural pronoun, many people now use it as a singular pronoun, in place of *he* or *she*: **If anyone comes to the door, tell them I'm not at home.** Some people disapprove of this use, but it is becoming very common in informal use. This is partly because there is no gender-neutral singular pronoun in English.

this here/these here/that there/them there Each of these phrases is nonstandard: *this here* for *this; these here* for *these; that there* for *that; them there* for *those.*

thusly/thus *Thusly* is a pointless synonym for *thus*. Speakers and writers often use *thusly* only for a deliberately humorous effect.

till/until/'til *Till* and *until* are used interchangeably in speech and writing; *'til*, a shortened form of *until*, is rarely used.

time period The expression *time period* is redundant, since *period* is a period of time: **The local ambulance squad reported three emergency calls in a one-week period** (not *time period*).

too Be careful when using *too* as an intensifier in speech and writing: **The dog is too mean.** Adding an explanation of the excessive quality makes the sentence more logical: **The dog is too mean to be trusted alone with children.**

toward/towards The two words are used interchangeably in both formal and informal speech and writing.

try and/try to While *try to* is the preferred form for formal speech and writing, both phrases occur in speech and informal writing.

type/type of In written English, *type of* is the preferred construction: **This is an unusual type of flower.** In informal speech and writing, it is acceptable to use *type* immediately before a noun: **I like this type car.**

used to could/used to be able to The phrase *used to could* is nonstandard for *used to be able to*: **I used to be able to** (not *used to could*) touch my toes.

very The adverb *very* is sometimes used unnecessarily, especially in modifying an absolute adjective: It was a **very** unique experience. In such instances, it clearly should be omitted. Further, *very* has become overworked and has lost much of its power. Use more precise modifiers such as *extremely* and *especially*.

want in/want out Both phrases are informal: *want in* for *want to enter*, *want out* for *want to leave*: The dog **wants to enter** (not *wants in*). The cat **wants to leave** (not *wants out*).

way/ways *Way* is the preferred usage for formal speech and writing; *ways* is used informally: They have a little **way** (not *ways*) to go before they reach the campground.

when/where *Where* and *when* are not interchangeable: Weekends are occasions **when** (not *where*) we have a chance to spend time with the family.

where at/where to Both phrases are generally considered to be too informal to be acceptable in good writing and formal speech: **Where** is John? (not *Where* is John *at?*) **Where** is Mike going? (not *Where* is Mike going *to?*)

where/that *Where* and *that* are not interchangeable: We see by the memo **that** (not *where*) overtime has been discontinued.

who/whoever; whom/whomever Traditionally, *who/ whoever* is used as a subject (the nominative case) and *whom/whomever* as an object (the objective case). In informal speech and writing, however, since *who* and *whom* often occur at the beginning of a sentence, people usually select *who*, regardless of grammatical function. The case distinction remains important in formal speech and writing.

without/unless *Without* as a conjunction is a dialectal or regional use of *unless*.

with regards to/with regard to/as regards/regarding Use *with regard to*, *regarding*, or *as regards* in place of *with regards to* in formal speech and writing: **As regards** your inquiry, we have asked our shipping department to hold the merchandise until Monday.

would have Do not use the phrase *would have* in place of *had* in clauses that begin with *if* and express a state contrary to fact: If the driver **had** (not *would have*) been wearing his seat belt, he would have escaped without injury.

would of/could of There is no such expression as *would of* or *could of*: He **would have** (not *would of*) gone. *Of* is not a substitute for *'ve*: She **would've** (not *would of*) left earlier.

you was *You was* is nonstandard for *you were*: **You were** (not *you was*) late on Thursday.

COMMONLY CONFUSED WORDS

Words are often confused if they have similar or identical forms or sounds. You may have the correct meaning in mind, but choosing the wrong word will change your expressed meaning. An *ingenuous* person is not the same as an *ingenious* person. Similarly, you may be using a word that is correct in a different context but does not express your intended meaning. To *infer* something is not the same as to *imply* it.

You may choose the wrong word because two words are identical or very similar in pronunciation but different in spelling. An example of a pair of words with the same pronunciation is *compliment, complement*. The confusion may arise from a small difference in spelling, as the pair *canvas, canvass*; or the homophones (words that sound alike) may be spelled quite differently, as the pairs *manor, manner* and *brake, break*. An example of a pair of words with similar but not identical pronunciation is *accept, except*; they are very different in usage and grammatical function.

Words may also be confused if they are spelled the same way but differ in meaning or in meaning and pronunciation, as the homophones *bear* "animal" and *bear* "carry, support" or the homographs (look-alike words) *row* (rō) "line" and *row* (rou) "fight."

Errors in word choice may also result if word groups overlap in meaning or usage. In informal contexts, *aggravate* may be used to mean "annoy" and *mad* may be used to mean "angry." *Leave* and *let* are interchangeable when followed by the word *alone* in the sense "to stop annoying or interfering with someone."

The following glossary lists words that are commonly confused and discusses their meanings and proper usage.

accept/except *Accept* is a verb meaning "to receive": **Please accept a gift.** *Except* is usually a preposition or a conjunction meaning "other than" or "but for": **He was willing to accept an apology from everyone except me.** When *except* is used as a verb, it means "to leave out": **He was excepted from the new regulations.**

accidentally/accidently The correct adverb is *accidentally*, from the root word *accidental*, not *accident*: **Russell accidentally slipped on the icy sidewalk.** *Accidently* is a misspelling.

adapt/adopt *Adapt* means "to adjust or modify to meet new needs": **He adapted the novel for the screen.** *Adopt* means "to take as one's own": **She adopted the nickname in high school. They adopted a child from Russia.** *Adopt* can also mean "to accept": **The Senate adopted the report.**

adoptive/adopted *Adoptive* refers to the parent: **He resembles his adoptive father.**

Adopted refers to the child: **Their adopted daughter wants to adopt a child herself.**

adverse/averse Both words are adjectives, and both mean "opposed" or "hostile." *Averse*, however, is used to describe a subject's opposition to something: **The minister was averse to the new trends developing in the country.** *Adverse* describes something opposed to the subject: **The adverse comments affected his self-esteem.**

advice/advise *Advice*, a noun, means "suggestion or suggestions": **Here's some good advice.** *Advise*, a verb, means "to offer ideas or suggestions": **Act as we advise you.**

affect/effect Most often, *affect* is a verb, meaning "to influence," and *effect* is a noun meaning "the result of an action": **His speech affected my mother very deeply, but had no effect on my sister at all.** *Affect* is also used as a noun in psychology and psychiatry to mean "emotion": **We can learn much about affect from performance.** In this usage, it is pronounced with the stress on the first syllable. *Effect* is also used as a verb meaning "to bring about": **His letter effected a change in their relationship.**

aggravate/annoy In informal speech and writing, *aggravate* can be used as a synonym for *annoy*. However, in formal discourse the words mean different things and should be used in this way: **Her back condition was aggravated by lifting the child, but the child's crying annoyed her more than the pain did.**

aisle/isle *Aisle* means "a passageway between sections of seats": **It was impossible to pass through the airplane aisle during the meal service.** *Isle* means "island": **I would like to be on a desert isle on such a dreary morning.**

all ready/already *All ready*, a pronoun and an adjective, means "entirely prepared"; *already*, an adverb, means "so soon" or "previously": **I was all ready to leave when I noticed that it was already dinnertime.**

allusion/illusion An *allusion* is a reference or hint: **He made an allusion to the past.** An *illusion* is a deceptive appearance: **The canals on Mars are an illusion.**

allude/elude Both words are verbs. *Allude* means "to mention briefly or accidentally": **During our conversation, he alluded to his vacation plans.** *Elude* means "to avoid or escape": **The thief has successfully eluded capture for six months.**

a lot/alot/allot *A lot* is always written as two words. It is used informally to mean "many": **The unrelenting heat frustrated a lot of people.** *Allot* is a verb meaning "to divide" or "to set aside": **We allotted a portion of the yard for a garden.**

Alot is not a word; it is a misspelling of *a lot*.

altar/alter *Altar* is a noun meaning "a sacred place or platform": **The couple approached the altar for the wedding ceremony.** *Alter* is a verb meaning "to make different; to change": **He altered his appearance by losing fifty pounds, growing a beard, and getting a new wardrobe.**

altogether/all together *Altogether* means "completely" or "totally"; *all together* means "all at one time" or "gathered together": **It is altogether proper that we recite the Pledge all together.**

amount/number *Amount* refers to quantity that cannot be counted: **The amount of work accomplished before a major holiday is always negligible.** *Number*, in contrast, refers to things that can be counted: **He has held a number of jobs in the past five months.** But some concepts, like time, can use either *amount* or *number*, depending how the elements are identified in the specific sentence: **We were surprised by the amount of time it took us to settle into our new surroundings. The number of hours it took to repair the sink pleased us.**

ante-/anti- The prefix *ante-* means "before": **antecedent, antechamber, antediluvian**; the prefix *anti-* means "against": **antigravity, antifreeze.** *Anti-* takes a hyphen before an *i* or a capital letter: **anti-Marxist, anti-inflationary**.

anxious/eager Traditionally, *anxious* means "nervous" or "worried" and consequently describes negative feelings. In addition, it is usually followed by the word *about*: **I'm anxious about** my exam. *Eager* means "looking forward" or "anticipating enthusiastically" and consequently describes positive feelings. It is usually followed by *to*: **I'm eager to hear their new CD**. Today, however, it is standard usage for *anxious* to mean "eager": **They are anxious to see their new home**.

anybody, any body/anyone, any one *Anybody* and *anyone* are pronouns; *any body* is a noun modified by *any* and *any one* is a pronoun or adjective modified by *any*. They are used as follows: **Was anybody** able to find **any body** in the debris? Will **anyone** help me? I have more cleaning than **any one** person can ever do.

any more/anymore *Any more* means "no more"; *anymore*, an adverb, means "nowadays" or "any longer": **We don't want any more trouble. We won't go there anymore**.

apt/likely *Apt* is standard in all speech and writing as a synonym for *likely* in suggesting chance without inclination: **They are apt to call any moment now**. *Likely*, meaning "probably," is frequently preceded by a qualifying word: **The new school budget will very likely raise taxes.** However, *likely* without the qualifying word is standard in all varieties of English: **The new school budget will likely raise taxes.**

ascent/assent *Ascent* is a noun that means "a move upward or a climb": **Their ascent up Mount Rainier was especially dangerous because of the recent rock slides.** *Assent* can be a noun or a verb. As a verb, *assent* means "to concur, to express agreement": **The union representative assented to the agreement.** As a noun, *assent* means "an agreement": **The assent was not reached peacefully.**

assistance/assistants *Assistance* is a noun that means "help, support": **Please give us your assistance here for a moment.** *Assistants* is a plural noun that means "helpers": **Since the assistants were late, we found ourselves running behind schedule.**

assure, ensure, insure *Assure* is a verb that means "to promise": **The plumber assured us that the sink would not clog again.** *Ensure* and *insure* are both verbs that mean "to make certain," although some writers use *insure* solely for legal and financial writing and *ensure* for more widespread usage: **Since it is hard to insure yourself against mudslide, we did not buy the house on the hill. We left**

late to **ensure** that we would not get caught in traffic.

bare/bear *Bare* is an adjective or a verb. As an adjective, *bare* means "naked, unadorned": **The wall looked bare** without the picture. As a verb, *bare* means "to reveal": **He bared his soul.** *Bear* is a noun or a verb. As a noun, *bear* refers to the animal: **The teddy bear was named after Theodore Roosevelt.** As a verb, *bear* means to carry: **He bears a heavy burden.**

before/prior to *Prior to* is used most often in formal contexts or in a legal sense: **Prior to settling the claim, the Smiths spent a week calling the attorney general's office.** Use *before* in almost all other cases: **Before we go grocery shopping, we sort the coupons we have clipped from the newspaper.**

beside/besides Although both words can function as prepositions, they have different shades of meaning: *beside* means "next to"; *besides* means "in addition to" or "except": **Besides, Richard would prefer not to sit beside the dog. There is no one here besides John and me.** *Besides* is also an adverb meaning "in addition": **Other people besides you feel the same way about the dog.**

bias/prejudice Generally, a distinction is made between *bias* and *prejudice*.

Although both words imply "a preconceived opinion" or a "subjective point of view" in favor of something or against it, *prejudice* is generally used to express unfavorable feelings.

blonde/blond A *blonde* indicates a woman or girl with fair hair and skin. *Blond,* as an adjective, refers to either sex: I have three **blond** children. He is a cute **blond** boy, but *blonde,* as an adjective, still applies only to women: The **blonde** actress and her companion made the front page of the tabloid.

borrow/lend *Borrow* means "to take with the intention of returning": The book you **borrow** from the library today is due back in seven days. *Lend* means "to give with the intention of getting back": I will **lend** you the rake, but I need it back by Saturday. The two terms are not interchangeable.

brake/break The most common meaning of *brake* as a noun is "a device for slowing a vehicle": The car's new **brakes** held on the steep incline. *Brake* can also mean "a thicket" or "a species of fern." *Break,* a verb, means "to crack or make useless": Please be especially careful that you don't **break** that vase.

breath/breathe *Breath,* a noun, is the air taken in during respiration: Her **breath** looked like fog in the frosty morning air. *Breathe,* a verb, refers to the process of inhaling and exhaling air: **"Please breathe deeply,"** the doctor said to the patient.

bring/take *Bring* is to carry toward the speaker: **She brings it to me.** *Take* is to carry away from the speaker: **She takes it away.**

buy/by *Buy*, a verb, means "to acquire goods at a price": **We have to buy a new dresser.** *By* can be a preposition, an adverb, or an adjective. As a preposition, *by* means "next to": **I pass by the office building every day.** As an adverb, *by* means "near, at hand": **The office is close by.** As an adjective, *by* means "situated to one side": **They came down on a by passage.**

canvas/canvass *Canvas*, a noun, refers to a heavy cloth: **The boat's sails are made of canvas.** *Canvass*, a verb, means "to solicit votes": **The candidate's representatives canvass the neighborhood seeking support.**

capital/Capitol *Capital* is the city or town that is the seat of government: **Paris is the capital of France.** *Capitol* refers to the building in Washington, D.C., in which the U.S. Congress meets: **When I was a child, we went for a visit to the Capitol.** When used with a lowercase letter, *capitol* is the building of a state legislature. *Capital* also means "a sum of money": **After the sale of their home, they had a great deal of**

capital. As an adjective, *capital* means "foremost" or "first-rate": **He was a capital fellow.**

censor/censure Both words are verbs, but they have different meanings. To *censor* is to remove something from public view on moral or other grounds, and to *censure* is to give a formal reprimand: **The committee censored the offending passages from the book and censured the librarian for placing it on the shelves.**

cite/sight/site *To cite* means to "quote a passage": **The scholar often cited passages from noted authorities to back up his opinions.** *Sight* is a noun that means "vision": **With her new glasses, her sight was once again perfect.** *Site* is a noun that means "place or location": **They picked out a beautiful site overlooking a lake for their new home.**

climatic/climactic The word *climatic* comes from the word *climate* and refers to weather: **This summer's brutal heat may indicate a climatic change.** *Climactic*, in contrast, comes from the word *climax* and refers to a point of high drama: **In the climactic last scene, the hideous creature takes over the world.**

clothes/cloths *Clothes* are garments: **For his birthday, John got some stylish new clothes.** *Cloths* are pieces of fabric: **Use these cloths to clean the car.**

coarse/course *Coarse*, an adjective, means "rough or common": The horsehair fabric was too **coarse** to be made into a pillow. Although his manners are a little **coarse**, he has a heart of gold. *Course*, a noun, means "a path" or "a prescribed number of classes": They followed the bicycle **course** through the woods. My **courses** include English, math, and science.

complement/compliment Both words can function as either a noun or a verb. The noun *complement* means "that which completes or makes perfect": The rich chocolate mousse was a perfect **complement** to the light meal. The verb *complement* means "to complete": The oak door **complemented** the new siding and windows. The noun *compliment* means "an expression of praise or admiration": The mayor paid the visiting officials the **compliment** of escorting them around town personally. The verb *compliment* means "to pay a compliment to": Everyone **complimented** her after the presentation.

complementary/complimentary *Complementary* is an adjective that means "forming a complement, completing": The **complementary** colors suited the mood of the room. *Complimentary* is an adjective that means "expressing a compliment": The **complimentary** reviews ensured the play a long run. *Complimentary* also means "free": We thanked them for the **complimentary** tickets.

continual/continuous Use *continual* to mean "intermittent, repeated often" and *continuous* to mean "uninterrupted, without stopping": We suffered **continual** losses of electricity during the hurricane. They had **continuous** phone service during the hurricane. *Continuous* and *continual* are never interchangeable with regard to spatial relationships: a **continuous** series of passages.

corps/corpse Both words are nouns. A *corps* is a group of people acting together; the word is often used in a military context: The officers' **corps** assembled before dawn for the drill. A *corpse* is a dead body: The **corpse** was in the morgue.

counsel/council *Counsel* is a verb meaning "to give advice": They **counsel** recovering gamblers. *Council* is a noun meaning "a group of advisers": The trade union **council** meets in Ward Hall every Thursday.

credible/creditable/credulous These three adjectives are often confused. *Credible* means "believable": The tale is unusual but seems **credible** to us. *Creditable* means "worthy": Sandra sang a **creditable** version of the song. *Credulous* means "gullible": The **credulous** boy believed that the movie was true.

demur/demure *Demur* is a verb meaning "to object": The board wanted her to be treasurer, but she **demurred**. *Demure* is an adjective meaning "modest" or "reserved:" Her response to their compliments was a **demure** smile.

descent/dissent *Descent*, a noun, means "downward movement": Much to their surprise, their **descent** down the mountain was harder than their ascent had been. *Dissent*, a verb, means "to disagree": The town council strongly **dissented** with the proposed measure. *Dissent* as a noun means "difference in sentiment or opinion": **Dissent** over the new proposal caused a rift between colleagues.

desert/dessert *Desert* as a verb means "to abandon"; as a noun, "an arid region": People **deserted** in the **desert** rarely survive. *Dessert*, a noun, refers to the sweet served as the final course of a meal: My sister's favorite **dessert** is strawberry shortcake.

device/devise *Device* is a noun meaning "invention or contrivance": Do you think that **device** will really save us time? *Devise* is a verb meaning "to contrive or plan": Did he **devise** some **device** for repairing the ancient pump assembly?

die/dye *Die*, as a verb, means "to cease to live": The frog will **die** if released from the aquarium into the pond. *Dye* as a verb means "to color or stain something": I **dyed** the drapes to cover the stains.

discreet/discrete *Discreet* means "tactful"; *discrete*, "separate." For example: Do you have a **discreet** way of refusing the invitation? The mosaic is made of hundreds of **discrete** pieces of tile.

disinterested/uninterested *Disinterested* is used to mean "without prejudice, impartial": He is a **disinterested** judge, and *uninterested* to mean "bored" or "lacking interest": They are completely **uninterested** in sports.

dominant/dominate *Dominant*, an adjective, means "ruling, controlling": Social scientists have long argued over the **dominant** motives for human behavior. *Dominate*, a verb, means "to control": Advice columnists often preach that no one can **dominate** you unless you allow them to.

elicit/illicit *Elicit*, a verb, means "call forth"; *illicit*, an adjective, means "against the law": The assault **elicited** a protest against **illicit** handguns.

emigrate/immigrate *Emigrate* means "to leave one's own country to settle in another": She **emigrated from** France. *Immigrate* means "to enter a different country and settle there": My father **immigrated to** America when he was nine years old.

eminent/imminent *Eminent* means "distinguished": Marie Curie was an **eminent** scientist who won the Nobel prize twice. *Imminent* means "about to happen": The thundershower seemed **imminent**.

envelop/envelope *Envelop* is a verb that means "to surround": The music **envelops** him in a soothing atmosphere. *Envelope*, a noun, is a flat paper container, usually for a letter: Be sure to put a stamp on the **envelope** before you mail that letter.

especially/specially The two words are not interchangeable: *especially* means "particularly," *specially* means "for a specific reason." For example: I **especially** value my wedding ring; it was made **specially** for me.

ever so often/every so often *Ever so often* means "happening very often" and *every so often* means "happening occasionally."

everybody, every body/everyone, every one *Everybody* and *everyone* are indefinite pronouns: **Everybody** likes William, and **everyone** enjoys his company. *Every body* is a noun modified by *every* and *every one* is a pronoun modified by *every*; both refer to a person in a specific group and are usually followed by *of*: **Every body** of water in our area is polluted; **every one** of our ponds is covered in debris.

everyday/every day *Everyday* is an adjective that means "used daily, typical, ordinary"; *every day* is made up of a noun modified by the adjective *every* and means "each day": **Every day they had to deal with the everyday business of life.**

exam/examination *Exam* should be reserved for every-day speech and *examination* for formal writing: **The SAT examinations are scheduled for this Saturday morning at 9:00.**

explicit/implicit *Explicit* means "stated plainly"; *implicit* means "understood, implied": **You know we have an implicit understanding that you are not allowed to visit Web sites that contain explicit sex.**

fair/fare *Fair* as an adjective means "free from bias," "ample," "unblemished," "of light hue," or "attractive." As an adverb, it means "favorably." It is used informally to mean "honest." *Fare* as a noun means "the price charged for transporting a person" or "food."

farther/further Traditionally, *farther* is used to indicate physical distance: **Is it much farther to the hotel?** and *further* is used to refer to additional time, amount, or abstract ideas: **Your mother does not want to talk about this any further.**

flaunt/flout *Flaunt* means "to show off"; *flout*, "to ignore or treat with disdain." For example: **They flouted convention when they flaunted their wealth.**

flounder/founder *Flounder* means "to struggle with clumsy movements": **We floundered in the mud.** *Founder* means "to sink": **The ship foundered.**

formally/formerly Both words are adverbs. *Formally* means "in a formal manner": **The minister addressed the king and queen formally.** *Formerly* means "previously": **Formerly, he worked as a chauffeur; now, he is employed as a guard.**

forth/fourth *Forth* is an adverb meaning "going forward or away": **From that day forth, they lived happily ever after.** *Fourth* is most often used as an adjective that means "next after the third": **Wyatt was the fourth in line.**

gibe/jibe/jive The word *gibe* means "to taunt; deride; jeer." The word *jibe* means "to be in agreement with; accord; correspond": **The facts of the case didn't jibe.** The word *jive* is slang and means "to tease; fool; kid."

healthy/healthful *Healthy* means "possessing health"; *healthful* means "bringing about health": **They believed that they were healthy people because they ate healthful food.**

historic/historical The word *historic* means "important in history": **a historic speech; a historic battlefield.** The word *historical* means "being a part of, or inspired by, history": **historical records; a historical novel.**

home in/hone in The expression *home in* means "to approach or focus on (an objective)." It comes from the language of guided missiles, where *homing in* refers to locking onto a target. The expression *hone in* is an error.

human/humane Both words are adjectives. *Human* means "pertaining to humanity": The subject of the documentary is the **human** race. *Humane* means "tender, compassionate, or sympathetic": Many of her patients believed that her **humane** care speeded their recovery.

idea/ideal *Idea* means "thought," while *ideal* means "a model of perfection" or "goal." The two words are not interchangeable. They should be used as follows: The **idea** behind the blood drive is that our **ideals** often move us to help others.

imply/infer *Imply* means "to suggest without stating": The message on Karen's postcard **implies** that her vacation has not turned out as she wished. *Infer* means "to reach a conclusion based on understood evidence": From her message I **infer** that she wishes she had stayed home. When used in this manner, the two words describe two sides of the same process.

incredible/incredulous *Incredible* means "cannot be believed"; *incredulous* means "unbelieving": The teacher was **incredulous** when she heard the pupil's **incredible** story about the fate of his term project.

individual/person/party *Individual* should be used to stress uniqueness or to refer to a single human being as contrasted to a group of people: The rights of the **individual** should not supersede the rights of a group. *Person* is the preferred word in other contexts. What **person** wouldn't want to have a chance to sail around the world? *Party* is used to refer to a group: Send the **party** of five this way, please. *Party* is also used to refer to an individual mentioned in a legal document.

ingenious/ingenuous *Ingenious* means "resourceful, clever": My sister is **ingenious** when it comes to turning leftovers into something delicious. *Ingenuous* means "frank, artless": The child's **ingenuous** manner is surprising considering her fame.

later/latter *Later* is used to refer to time; *latter*, the second of two items named: It is **later** than you think. Of the two shirts I just purchased, I prefer the **latter**.

lay/lie *Lay* is a transitive verb that means "to put down" or "to place." It takes a direct object: Please **lay** the soup spoon next to the teaspoon. *Lie* is an intransitive verb that means "to be in a horizontal position" or "be situated." It does not take a direct object: **The puppy lies down where the old dog had always lain. The hotel lies on the outskirts of town.** The confusion arises over *lay*, which is the present tense of the verb *lay* and the past tense of the verb *lie*.

To lie (recline)

Present: Spot **lies (is lying)** down.

Future: Spot **will lie** down.

Past: Spot **lay** down.

Perfect: Spot **has (had, will have) lain** down.

To lay (put down)

Present: He **lays (is laying)** his dice down.

Future: He **will lay** his dice down.

Past: He **laid** his dice down.

Perfect: He **has (had, will have) laid** his dice down.

Although *lie* and *lay* are used interchangeably by many people, phrases such as the following are considered nonstandard and should be avoided: **Lay down, dears. The dog laid in the sun. Abandoned cars were laying in the junkyard. The reports have laid in the mailbox for a week.**

lead/led *Lead* as a verb means "to take or conduct on the way": I plan to **lead** a quiet afternoon. *Led* is the past tense: He **led** his followers through the dangerous underbrush. *Lead*, as a noun, means "a type of metal": Pipes are made of **lead**.

learn/teach *Learn* is to acquire knowledge: He **learned** fast. *Teach* is to impart knowledge: She **taught** well. The two words describe two sides of the same process and are not interchangeable.

leave/let *Leave* and *let* are interchangeable only when followed by the word *alone*: **Leave** him alone. **Let** him alone. In other instances, *leave* means "to depart" or "permit to remain in the same place": If you **leave**, please turn off the copier. **Leave** the extra paper on the shelf. *Let* means "to allow": **Let** him work with the assistant, if he wants.

lessen/lesson *Lessen* is a verb meaning "to decrease": To **lessen** the pain of a burn, apply ice to the injured area. *Lesson* is most often used as a noun meaning "material assigned for study": Today, the **lesson** will be on electricity.

lightening/lightning *Lightening* is a form of the verb that means "to brighten": The cheerful new drapes and bunches of flowers went a long way in **lightening** the room's somber mood. *Lightning* is most often used as a noun to mean "flashes of light generated during a storm": The thunder and **lightning** frightened the child.

loose/lose *Loose* as an adjective means "free and unattached": The dog was

loose again. *Loose* can also be a verb meaning "let loose": **The hunters loose the dogs as soon as the ducks fall.** *Lose* is a verb meaning "to part with unintentionally": **He will lose his keys if he leaves them on the countertop.**

mad/angry Traditionally, *mad* has been used to mean "insane"; *angry* has been used to mean "full of ire." While *mad* can be used to mean "enraged, angry," in informal usage, you should replace *mad* with *angry* in formal discourse: **The president is angry at Congress for overriding his veto.**

maybe/may be *Maybe*, an adverb, means "perhaps": **Maybe the newspapers can be recycled with the plastic and glass.** *May be*, a verb, means "could be": **It may be too difficult, however.**

moral/morale As a noun, *moral* means "ethical lesson": **Each of Aesop's fables has a clear moral.** *Morale* means "state of mind" or "spirit": **Her morale was lifted by her colleague's good wishes.**

orient/orientate The two words both mean "to adjust to or familiarize with new surroundings; place in a particular position." There is no reason to prefer or reject either word; however, some people object to *orientate*, so *orient* is a safer choice in a conservative writing situation.

passed/past *Passed* is a form of the verb meaning "to go by": **Bernie passed the**

same buildings on his way to work each day. *Past* can function as a noun, adjective, adverb, or preposition. As a noun, *past* means "the history of a nation, person, etc.": **The lessons of the past should not be forgotten.** As an adjective, *past* means "gone by or elapsed in time": **John is worried about his past deeds.** As an adverb, *past* means "so as to pass by": **The fire engine raced past the parked cars.** As a preposition, *past* means "beyond in time": **It's past noon already.**

patience/patients *Patience*, a noun, means "endurance": **Antonella's patience makes her an ideal baby-sitter.** *Patients* are people under medical treatment: **The patients must remain in the hospital for another week.**

peace/piece *Peace* is "freedom from discord": **The negotiators hoped that the new treaty would bring about lasting peace.** *Piece* is "a portion of a whole" or "a short musical arrangement": **I would like just a small piece of cake, please. The piece in E flat is especially beautiful.**

percent/percentage *Percent* is used with a number, *percentage* with a modifier. *Percentage* is used most often after an adjective: **A high percentage of your earnings this year is tax deductible.**

personal/personnel *Personal* means "private": **Your question is an unacceptable**

intrusion into my **personal** affairs. *Personnel* refers to employees: **Attention all personnel!** The use of *personnel* as a plural has become standard in business and government: **The personnel were dispatched to the Chicago office.**

plain/plane *Plain* as an adjective means "easily understood," "undistinguished," or "unadorned": **His meaning was plain to all. The plain dress suited the gravity of the occasion.** As an adverb, *plain* means "clearly and simply": **She's just plain foolish.** As a noun, *plain* is a flat area of land: **The vast plain seemed to go on forever.** As a noun, *plane* has a number of different meanings. It most commonly refers to an *airplane*, but is also used in mathematics and fine arts and to refer to a tool used to shave wood.

practicable/practical *Practicable* means "capable of being done": **My decorating plans were too difficult to be practicable.** *Practical* means "pertaining to practice or action": **It was just not practical to paint the floor white.**

precede/proceed Both words are verbs, but they have different meanings. *Precede* means "to go before": **Morning precedes afternoon.** *Proceed* means "to move forward": **Proceed to the exit in an orderly fashion.**

presence/presents *Presence* is used chiefly to mean "attendance, close proximity":

Your **presence** at the ceremony will be greatly appreciated. *Presents* are gifts. Thank you for giving us such generous **presents**.

principal/principle *Principal* can be a noun or an adjective. As a noun, *principal* means "chief or head official": **The principal decided to close school early on Tuesday**, or "sum of capital": **Invest only the interest, never the principal.** As an adjective, *principal* means "first or highest": **The principal ingredient is sugar.** *Principle* is a noun only, meaning "rule" or "general truth": **Regardless of what others said, she stood by her principles.**

quiet/quite *Quiet*, as an adjective, means "free from noise": **When the master of ceremonies spoke, the room became quiet.** *Quite*, an adverb, means "completely, wholly": **By the late afternoon, the children were quite exhausted.**

quotation/quote *Quotation*, a noun, means "a passage quoted from a speech or book": **The speaker read a quotation of twenty-five lines to the audience.** *Quote*, a verb, means "to repeat a passage from a speech, etc.": **Marci often quotes from popular novels.** *Quote* and *quotation* are often used interchangeably in speech; in formal writing, however, a distinction is still observed between the two words.

rain/reign/rein As a noun, *rain* means "water that falls from the atmosphere to earth." As a verb, *rain* means "to send down, to give abundantly": **The crushed piñata rained candy on the eager children.** As a noun, *reign* means "royal rule," as a verb, "to have supreme control": **The monarch's reign was marked by social unrest.** As a noun, *rein* means "a leather strap used to guide an animal," as a verb, "to control or guide": **He used the rein to control the frisky colt.**

raise/rise/raze *Raise*, a transitive verb, means "to elevate": **How can I raise the price of my house?** *Rise*, an intransitive verb, means "to go up, to get up": **Will housing costs rise this year?** *Raze* is a transitive verb meaning "to tear down, demolish": **The wrecking crew was ready to raze the condemned building.**

respectful/respective *Respectful* means "showing (or full of) respect": **If you are respectful toward others, they will treat you with consideration as well.** *Respective* means "in the order given": **The respective remarks were made by executive board members Joshua Whittles, Kevin McCarthy, and Warren Richmond.**

reverend/reverent As an adjective (usually capitalized) *Reverend* is an epithet of respect given to a member of the clergy: **The Reverend Mr. Williams gave the sermon.** As a noun, a reverend is "a member of the clergy": **In our church, the reverend opens the service with a prayer.**

Reverent is an adjective meaning "showing deep respect": **The speaker addressed the princess with a reverent greeting.**

right/rite/write *Right* as an adjective means "proper, correct" and "as opposed to left," as a noun it means "claims or titles," as an adverb it means "in a straight line, directly," as a verb it means "to restore to an upright position." *Rite* is a noun meaning "a solemn ritual": **The religious leader performed the necessary rites.** *Write* is a verb meaning "to form characters on a surface": **The child liked to write her name over and over.**

sensual/sensuous *Sensual* carries sexual overtones: **The massage was a sensual experience.** *Sensuous* means "pertaining to the senses": **The sensuous aroma of freshly baked bread wafted through the house.**

set/sit *Set*, a transitive verb, describes something a person does to an object: **She set the book down on the table.** *Sit*, an intransitive verb, describes a person or thing resting: **Carlos sits on the straight-backed chair.**

somebody/some body *Somebody* is an indefinite pronoun: **Somebody recommended this restaurant.** *Some body* is a noun modified by an adjective: **I have a new spray that will give my limp hair some body.**

someone/some one *Someone* is an indefinite pronoun: **Someone who ate here said the pasta was delicious.** *Some one* is a pronoun or adjective modified by *some*: **Please pick some one magazine that you would like to read.**

sometime/sometimes/some time Traditionally, these three words have carried different meanings. *Sometime* means "at an unspecified time in the future": **Why not plan to visit Niagara Falls sometime?** *Sometimes* means "occasionally": **I visit my former college roommate sometimes.** *Some time* means "a span of time": **I need some time to make up my mind about what you have said.**

stationary/stationery These two words sound alike, but they have very different meanings. *Stationary* means "staying in one place": **From this distance, the satellite appeared to be stationary.** *Stationery* means "writing paper": **A hotel often provides stationery with its name preprinted.**

straight/strait *Straight* is most often used as an adjective meaning "unbending": **The path cut straight through the woods.** *Strait*, a noun, is "a narrow passage of water connecting two large bodies of water" or "distress, dilemma": **He was in dire financial straits.**

subsequently/consequently *Subsequently* means "occurring later, afterward": **We**

went to a new French restaurant for dinner; **subsequently,** we heard that everyone who had eaten the Caesar salad became ill. *Consequently* means "therefore, as a result": The temperature was above 90 degrees for a week; **consequently** all the tomatoes burst on the vine.

taught/taut *Taught* is the past tense of *to teach*: My English teachers **taught** especially well. *Taut* means "tightly drawn": Pull the knot **taut** or it will not hold.

than/then *Than*, a conjunction, is used in comparisons: Robert is taller **than** Michael. *Then*, an adverb, is used to indicate time: We knew **then** that there was little to be gained by further discussion.

their/there/they're These three words sound alike, but they have very different meanings. *Their*, the possessive form of *they*, means "belonging to them": **Their** house is new. *There* can point out place: **There** is the picture I was telling you about, or call attention to someone or something: **There** is a mouse behind you! *They're* is a contraction for *they are*: **They're** not at home right now.

threw/thru/through *Threw*, the past tense of the verb *throw*, means "to hurl an object": He **threw** the ball at the batter. *Through* means "from one end to the other" or "by way of": They walked **through** the museum all afternoon. *Through* should be used in formal writing in place of *thru*, an informal spelling.

to/too/two Although the words sound alike, they are different parts of speech and have different meanings. *To* is a preposition indicating direction or part of an infinitive; *too* is an adverb meaning "also" or "in extreme"; and *two* is a number: I have **to** go **to** the store **to** buy **two** items. Do you want **to** come **too**?

track/tract *Track*, as a noun, is a path or course: The railroad **track** in the Omaha station has recently been electrified. *Track*, as a verb, is "to follow": Sophisticated guidance control systems are used to **track** the space shuttles. *Tract* is "an expanse of land" or "a brief treatise": Jonathan Swift wrote many **tracts** on the political problems of his day.

unexceptional/unexceptionable Both *unexceptional* and *unexceptionable* are adjectives, but they have different meanings and are not interchangeable. *Unexceptional* means "commonplace, ordinary": Despite the glowing reviews the new restaurant had received, we found it offered **unexceptional** meals and service. *Unexceptionable* means "not offering any basis for exception or objection, beyond criticism": We could not dispute his argument because it was **unexceptionable**.

usage/use *Usage* is a noun that refers to the generally accepted way of doing something. The word refers especially to the conventions of language: **"Most unique" is considered incorrect usage.** *Use* can be either a noun or a verb. As a noun, *use* means "the act of employing or putting into service": **In the adult education course, I learned the correct use of tools.** *Usage* is often misused in place of the noun *use*: **Effective use** (not *usage*) **of your time results in greater personal satisfaction.**

use/utilize/utilization *Utilize* means "to make use of": **They should utilize the new profit-sharing plan to decrease taxable income.** *Utilization* is the noun form of *utilize*. In most instances, however, *use* is preferred to either *utilize* or *utilization* as less overly formal and stilted: **They should use the new profit-sharing plan to decrease taxable income.**

which/witch *Which* is a pronoun meaning "what one": **Which desk is yours?** *Witch* is a noun meaning "a person who practices magic": **The superstitious villagers accused her of being a witch.**

who's/whose *Who's* is the contraction for *who is* or *who has*: **Who's the person in charge here? Who's got the money?** *Whose* is the possessive form of *who*: **Whose book is this?**

your/you're *Your* is the possessive form of *you*: **Your book is overdue at the library.** *You're* is the contraction of *you are*: **You're just the person we need for this job.**

AVOIDING INSENSITIVE AND OFFENSIVE LANGUAGE

This essay is intended as a general guide to language that can, intentionally or not, cause offense or perpetuate discriminatory values and practices by emphasizing the differences between people or implying that one group is superior to another. Its purpose is to make readers aware of the possible consequences of the words they choose. Before looking at the words themselves, it is important to note that offensive or insensitive speech is not limited to a specific group of words. One can be hurtful and insulting by using any type of vocabulary, if that is one's intent. While in most cases it is easy to avoid blatantly offensive slurs and comments, more subtle bias that is an inherent part of our language or that is the habit of a lifetime is much harder to change.

Several factors complicate the issue. A group may disagree within itself as to what is acceptable and what is not. Many seemingly inoffensive terms develop negative connotations over time and become dated or go out of style as awareness changes. A "within the group" rule often applies, which allows a member of a group to use terms freely that would be considered offensive if used by a non-member of the group.

What is considered acceptable shifts constantly as people become more aware of language and its power. The rapid changes of the last few decades have left many people puzzled and afraid of unintentionally insulting someone. At the same time, these changes have angered others, who decry what they see as extremes of "political correctness" in rules and locutions that alter language to the point of obscuring, even destroying, its meaning. The abandonment of traditional usages has also upset many people. But while it is true that some of the more extreme attempts to avoid offending language have resulted in ludicrous obfuscation, it is also true that heightened sensitivity in language is a statement of respect, indicates precision of thought, and is a positive move toward rectifying the unequal social status between one group and another.

Suggestions for avoiding language that reinforces stereotypes or excludes certain groups of people are given in the following pages. In each case the suggested terms are given on the right. While these suggestions can reflect trends, they cannot dictate or predict the preferences of each individual.

SEXISM

Sexism is the most difficult bias to avoid, in part because of the convention of using *man* or *men* and *he* or *his* to refer to people of either sex. Other, more disrespectful conventions include giving descriptions of women in terms of age and appearance while describing men in terms of accomplishment, and neglecting to use parallel terms to refer to men and women. Some suggestions for avoiding sexism in language are given below.

REPLACING *MAN* OR *MEN*

Man may refer to a male or to a human in general. This ambiguity is often thought to be slighting of women.

mankind, man	human beings, humans, human-kind, humanity, people, human race, human species, homo sapiens, society, men and women
a man who	someone who, anyone who
man-made	synthetic, artificial
man in the street	average person, ordinary person

USING GENDER-NEUTRAL TERMS FOR OCCUPATIONS, POSITIONS, ROLES, ETC.

Terms that specify or imply a particular sex can unnecessarily perpetuate certain stereotypes when used generically.

anchorman	anchor
bellman, bellboy	bellhop

businessman	businessperson, business executive, manager, business owner, retailer, etc.
chairman	chair, chairperson
cleaning lady, girl, maid	housecleaner, housekeeper, cleaning person, office cleaner
clergyman	member of the clergy, minister, rabbi, priest, pastor, etc.
clergymen	the clergy
congressman	representative, member of Congress, legislator
fireman	firefighter
forefather	ancestor
girl/gal Friday	assistant
housewife	homemaker
insurance man	insurance agent
layman	layperson, nonspecialist, nonprofessional
mailman, postman	mail carrier, letter carrier
policeman	police officer, law enforcement officer
salesman, saleswoman, saleslady, salesgirl	salesperson, sales representative, sales associate, clerk

spokesman	spokesperson, representative,
stewardess, steward	flight attendant
weatherman	weather reporter, weathercaster, meteorologist
workman	worker
actress	actor

AVOIDING THE GENERIC USE OF THE PERSONAL PRONOUNS *HE, HIS,* AND *HIM*

Like man, he can be used both generically and referring to males. The generic use can be seen to exclude women.

When a driver approaches a red light, he must prepare to stop.	When drivers approach a red light, they must prepare to stop.
	When a driver approaches a red light, he or she must prepare to stop.
	When approaching a red light, a driver must prepare to stop.
	A driver must prepare to stop when approaching a red light.

Man's natural rights are the foundation of all his civil rights.	The natural rights of human beings are the foundation of all their civil rights.

REFERRING TO MEMBERS OF BOTH SEXES WITH PARALLEL NAMES, TITLES, OR DESCRIPTIONS

Don't be inconsistent unless you are trying to make a specific point.

men and ladies	men and women, ladies and gentlemen
10 men and 13 females	10 men and 13 women
Betty Schmidt, an attractive 49-year-old physcian, and her husband, Alan Schmidt, a noted editor	Betty Schmidt, a physician, and her husband, Alan Schmidt, a noted editor
Mr. David Kim and Mrs. Betty Harrow	Mr. David Kim and Ms. Betty Harrow (unless Mrs. is her known preference)
man and wife	husband and wife
Dear Sir:	Dear Sir/Madam: Dear Madam or Sir: To whom it may concern:

Mrs. Smith and	Governor Smith
President Jones	and President
	Jones

RACE, ETHNICITY, AND NATIONAL ORIGIN

Some words and phrases that refer to racial and ethnic groups are clearly offensive. Other words (e.g., *Indian, Oriental, colored*) are outdated or inaccurate. *Hispanic* is generally accepted as a broad term for Spanish-speaking people of the Western Hemisphere, but more specific terms (*Latino, Mexican American, Cuban American*) are also acceptable and in some cases preferred. *Mixed race* and *multiracial* are acceptable terms for people who identify with more than one race.

Negro, colored, Afro-American	black, African-American (generally preferred to Afro-American)
Oriental, Asiatic	Asian, or more specific designations such as Pacific Islander, Chinese American, Korean
Indian	Indian properly refers to people who live in or hail from India.

	American Indian, Native American, or more specific designations (Chinook, Hopi), are usually preferred when referring to the native peoples of the Western Hemisphere.
Eskimo	Inuit, Alaska natives
native (noun)	native peoples, early inhabitants, aboriginal peoples (but not aborigines)

AGE

The concept of aging is changing as people are living longer and more active lives. Be aware of word choices that reinforce stereotypes (*decrepit, senile*) and avoid mentioning age unless it is relevant to the subject at hand. As with other groups, preferred terms for referring to older people are changing, and individual preferences may vary.

elderly, aged, old, geriatric, the elderly, the aged	older person, senior citizen, older people, senior citizens, seniors

SEXUAL ORIENTATION

The term *homosexual* to describe a man or a woman is increasingly replaced by the terms *gay* for men and *lesbian* for women. Among homosexuals, certain terms (such as *queer* and *dyke*) that are usually considered offensive have been gaining currency in recent years, particularly among radicals and in the academic community. However, it is still prudent to avoid these terms in standard contexts. The term *life partner* is frequently used when referring to one member of a committed gay relationship as well as to members of heterosexual relationships. *Sexual orientation* has replaced *sexual preference*, which implies choice. In some contexts, *same-sex* is appropriate: *same-sex marriage, same-sex parents.*

AVOIDING DEPERSONALIZATION OF PERSONS WITH DISABILITIES OR ILLNESSES

Terminology that emphasizes the person rather than the disability is generally preferred when referring to a person with a physical or mental impairment or disability. *Handicap* is used to refer to the environmental barrier that affects the person. (Stairs handicap a person who uses a wheelchair.) While words such as *crazy, demented*, and *insane* are used in facetious or informal contexts, these terms are no longer in technical use and are not used to describe people with clinical diagnoses of mental illness. The euphemisms *challenged, differently abled*, and *special* are preferred by some people, but are often ridiculed and are best avoided.

Mongoloid	person with Down syndrome
wheelchair-bound	a person who uses a wheelchair
AIDS sufferer, person afflicted with AIDS, AIDS victim	person with AIDS, P.W.A., HIV+ (someone who tests positive for HIV but does not yet show symptoms of AIDS)
polio victim	has/had polio
the handicapped, the disabled, cripple	persons with disabilities, person with a disability or person who uses crutches or other more specific description
deaf-mute, deaf and dumb	deaf person

AVOIDING PATRONIZING OR DEMEANING EXPRESSIONS

These are expressions that can offend, regardless of intention.

girls (when referring to adult women), the fair sex	women
sweetie, dear, dearie, honey	(usually not appropriate with strangers or in public situations)
old maid, spinster, bachelorette	single woman, woman, divorced woman (but only if one would specify "divorced man" in the same context)
the little woman, old lady, ball and chain	wife
boy (when referring to or addressing an adult man)	man, sir

AVOIDING LANGUAGE THAT EXCLUDES OR UNNECESSARILY EMPHASIZES DIFFERENCES

Expressions that can offend, regardless of intention. References to age, sex, religion, race, and the like should only be included if they are relevant.

lawyers and their wives	lawyers and their spouses

a secretary and her boss	a secretary and boss, a secretary and his or her boss
a good female surgeon	a good surgeon
the male nurse	the nurse
Arab man denies assault charge	Man denies assault charge
the articulate black student	the articulate student
Marie Curie was a great woman scientist	Marie Curie was a great scientist. (unless the intent is to compare her only with other women in the sciences)
Christian name	given name, personal name, first name
Mr. Johnson, the black representative, met with the President today to discuss civil-rights legislation.	Mr. Johnson, a member of the Congressional Black Caucus, met with the President today to discuss civil-rights legislation.

Spelling

SPELLING RULES

Correct spelling is an important part of correct usage. English spellings present some difficulties because so many words are not spelled the way they sound. The following rules can serve as general guidelines. Remember that no spelling rule should be followed blindly because every rule has its exceptions.

1. Silent *E* Dropped. Silent *e* at the end of a word is usually dropped before a suffix beginning with a vowel: *abide, abiding; recite, recital.*

   Exceptions: Words ending in *ce* or *ge* retain the *e* before a suffix beginning with *a* or *o* to keep the soft sound of the consonant: *notice, noticeable; courage, courageous.*

2. Silent *E* Kept. A silent *e* following a consonant (or another *e*) is usually retained before a suffix beginning with a consonant: *late, lateness; spite, spiteful.*

   Exceptions: *fledgling, acknowledgment, judgment, wholly,* and a few similar words.

3. Final Consonant Doubled. A final consonant following a single vowel in one-syllable words, or in a syllable that will take the main accent when combined with a suffix, is doubled before a suffix begin-

ning with a vowel: *begin*, *beginning*;
occur, *occurred*; *bat*, *batted*.

Exceptions: *h* and *x* in final position;
transferable, *gaseous*, and a few others.

4. Final Consonant Single. A final consonant following another consonant, a
   double vowel or diphthong, or that is not
   in a stressed syllable, is not doubled
   before a suffix beginning with a vowel:
   part, *parting*; remark, *remarkable*.

   Exceptions: an unaccented syllable does
   not prevent doubling of the final consonant, especially in British usage: *traveller*
   for *traveler*.

5. Double Consonants Remain. Double consonants are usually retained before a suffix except when a final *l* is to be followed
   by *ly* or *less*. To avoid a triple *lll*, one *l* is
   usually dropped: *full*, *fully*.

   Exceptions: Usage is divided, with some
   preferring *skilful* over *skillful*, *instalment*
   over *installment*, etc.

6. Final Y. If the *y* follows a consonant,
   change *y* to *i* before all endings except
   ing. Do not change it before *ing* or if it
   follows a vowel: *bury*, *buried*, *burying*;
   try, *tries*; but *attorney*, *attorneys*.

   Exceptions: day, *daily*; gay, *gaily*; lay,
   laid; say, *said*.

7. Final IE to Y. Words ending in *ie* change
   to *y* before *ing*: *die*, *dying*; *lie*, *lying*

8. **Double and Triple *E* Reduced.** Words ending in double *e* drop one *e* before an ending beginning in *e*, to avoid a triple *e*. Words ending in silent *e* usually drop the *e* before endings beginning in *e* to avoid forming a syllable. Other words ending in a vowel sound commonly retain the letters indicating the sound. *Free + ed = freed.*

9. ***EI* or *IE*.** Words having the sound of *ē* are commonly spelled *ie* following all letters but *c*; with a preceding *c*, the common spelling is *ei*. Examples: *believe, achieve, besiege*; but *conceit, ceiling, receive, conceive*. When the sound is *ā* the common spelling is *ei* regardless of the preceding letter. Examples: *eight, weight, deign.*

   Exceptions: *either, neither, seize, financier*; some words in which *e* and *i* are pronounced separately, such as *notoriety*.

10. **Words Ending in *C*.** Before an ending beginning with *e, i,* or *y*, words ending in *c* commonly add *k* to keep the *c* hard: *panic, panicky.*

11. **Compounds.** Some compounds written as a unit bring together unusual combinations of letters. They are seldom changed on this account: *bookkeeper, roommate.*

   Exceptions: A few words are regularly clipped when compounded, such as *full* in *awful, cupful,* etc.

WORDS COMMONLY MISSPELLED

aberrant
abscess
absence
absorption
abundance
accede
acceptance
accessible
accidentally
accommodate
according
accordion
accumulate
accustom
achievement
acknowledge
acknowledg-
ment
acoustics
acquaintance
acquiesce
acquire
acquittal
across
address
adequate
adherent
adjourn
admittance

adolescence
adolescent
advantageous
advertisement
affidavit
against
aggravate
aggression
aging
aisle
alien
all right
allegiance
almost
already
although
always
amateur
analysis
analytical
analyze
anesthetic
annual
anoint
anonymous
answer
Antarctic
antecedent
anticipation

antihistamine
anxiety
aperitif
apocryphal
apostasy
apparent
appearance
appetite
appreciate
appropriate
approximate
apropos
arctic
arguing
argument
arouse
arrangement
arthritis
article
artificial
asinine
asked
assassin
assess
asthma
athlete
athletic
attorneys
author
authoritative
auxiliary
bachelor
balance

bankruptcy
barbiturate
barrette
basically
basis
beggar
beginning
belief
believable
believe
beneficial
beneficiary
benefit
benefited
blizzard
bludgeon
bologna
bookkeeping
bouillon
boundaries
braggadocio
breathe
brief
brilliant
broccoli
bronchial
brutality
bulletin
buoy
buoyant
bureau
bureaucracy
burglary

business
cafeteria
caffeine
calisthenics
camaraderie
camouflage
campaign
cancel
cancellation
candidate
cantaloupe
capacity
cappuccino
carburetor
career
careful
carriage
carrying
casserole
category
caterpillar
cavalry
ceiling
cellar
cemetery
census
certain
challenge
chandelier
changeable
changing
characteristic
chief

choir
choose
cinnamon
circuit
civilized
clothes
codeine
collateral
colloquial
colonel
colossal
column
coming
commemorate
commission
commitment
committed
committee
comparative
comparison
competition
competitive
complaint
concede
conceivable
conceive
condemn
condescend
conferred
confidential
congratulate
conscience
conscientious

conscious
consensus
consequently
consistent
consummate
continuous
control
controlled
controversy
convalesce
convenience
coolly
copyright
cornucopia
corollary
corporation
correlate
correspondence
correspondent
counselor
counterfeit
courageous
courteous
crisis
criticism
criticize
culinary
curiosity
curriculum
cylinder
debt
debtor
deceive

decide
decision
decisive
defendant
definite
definitely
dependent
de rigueur
descend
descendant
description
desiccate
desirable
despair
desperate
destroy
develop
development
diabetes
diaphragm
different
dilemma
dining
diocese
diphtheria
disappear
disappearance
disappoint
disastrous
discipline
disease
dissatisfied
dissident

dissipate
distinguish
divide
divine
doesn't
dormitory
duly
dumbbell
during
easier
easily
ecstasy
effervescent
efficacy
efficiency
efficient
eighth
eightieth
electrician
eligibility
eligible
eliminate
ellipsis
embarrass
encouraging
endurance
energetic
enforceable
enthusiasm
environment
equipped
erroneous
especially

esteemed
exacerbate
exaggerate
exceed
excel
excellent
except
exceptionally
excessive
executive
exercise
exhibition
exhilarate
existence
expense
experience
experiment
explanation
exquisite
extemporaneous
extraordinary
extremely
facilities
fallacy
familiar
fascinate
fascism
feasible
February
fictitious
fiend
fierce
fiftieth

finagle
finally
financial
fluorine
foliage
forcible
forehead
foreign
forfeit
formally
forte
fortieth
fortunately
forty
fourth
friend
frieze
fundamental
furniture
galoshes
gauge
genealogy
generally
gnash
government
governor
graffiti
grammar
grateful
grievance
grievous
guarantee
guard

guidance
handkerchief
haphazard
harass
harebrained
hazard
height
hemorrhage
hemorrhoid
hereditary
heroes
hierarchy
hindrance
hoping
hors d'oeuvres
huge
humorous
hundredth
hurrying
hydraulic
hygiene
hygienist
hypocrisy
icicle
identification
idiosyncrasy
imaginary
immediately
immense
impostor
impresario
inalienable
incident

incidentally
inconvenience
incredible
indelible
independent
indestructible
indictment
indigestible
indispensable
inevitable
inferred
influential
initial
initiative
innocuous
innuendo
inoculation
inscrutable
installation
instantaneous
intellectual
intelligence
intercede
interest
interfere
intermittent
intimate
inveigle
irrelevant
irresistible
island
jealous
jeopardize

journal
judgment
judicial
khaki
kindergarten
knowledge
laboratory
laid
larynx
leery
leisure
length
liable
liaison
libel
library
license
lieutenant
lightning
likelihood
liquefy
liqueur
literature
livelihood
loneliness
losing
lovable
magazine
maintenance
manageable
management
maneuver
manufacturer

maraschino
marital
marriage
marriageable
mathematics
mayonnaise
meant
medicine
medieval
memento
mileage
millennium
miniature
minuet
miscellaneous
mischievous
misspell
mistletoe
moccasin
molasses
molecule
monotonous
mortgage
murmur
muscle
mutual
mysterious
naive
naturally
necessarily
necessary
necessity
neighbor

neither
nickel
niece
ninetieth
ninety
ninth
noticeable
notoriety
nuptial
obbligato
occasion
occasionally
occurred
occurrence
offense
official
omission
omit
omitted
oneself
ophthalmology
opinion
opportunity
optimism
optimist
ordinarily
origin
original
outrageous
paean
pageant
paid
pamphlet

paradise	philosophy
parakeet	physician
parallel	piccolo
paralysis	plaited
paralyze	plateau
paraphernalia	plausible
parimutuel	playwright
parliament	pleasant
partial	plebeian
participate	pneumonia
particularly	poinsettia
pasteurize	politician
pastime	pomegranate
pavilion	possess
peaceable	possession
peasant	possibility
peculiar	possible
penicillin	practically
perceive	practice
perform	precede
performance	precedence
peril	precisely
permanent	predecessor
permissible	preference
perpendicular	preferred
perseverance	prejudice
persistent	preparatory
personnel	prescription
perspiration	prevalent
persuade	primitive
persuasion	prior
persuasive	privilege
petition	probability

probably
procedure
proceed
professor
proffer
pronounce
pronunciation
propagate
protégé(e)
psychiatry
psychology
pursuant
pursue
pursuit
putrefy
quantity
questionnaire
queue
rarefy
recede
receipt
receivable
receive
recipe
reciprocal
recognize
recommend
reference
referred
reign
relegate
relevant
relieve

religious
remembrance
reminisce
remiss
remittance
rendezvous
repetition
replaceable
representative
requisition
resistance
responsibility
restaurant
restaurateur
resuscitate
reticence
reveille
rhyme
rhythm
riddance
ridiculous
rococo
roommate
sacrifice
sacrilegious
safety
salary
sandwich
sarsaparilla
sassafras
satisfaction
scarcity
scene

scenery
schedule
scheme
scholarly
scissors
secede
secrecy
secretary
seize
seizure
separate
separately
sergeant
serviceable
seventieth
several
sheik
shepherd
sheriff
shining
shoulder
shrapnel
siege
sieve
significance
silhouette
similar
simultaneity
simultaneous
sincerely
sixtieth
skiing
socially

society
solemn
soliloquy
sophomore
sorority
sovereign
spaghetti
spatial
special
specifically
specimen
speech
sponsor
spontaneous
statistics
statute
stevedore
stiletto
stopped
stopping
strength
strictly
studying
stupefy
submitted
substantial
subtle
subtly
succeed
successful
succession
successive
sufficient

superintendent
supersede
supplement
suppress
surprise
surveillance
susceptible
suspicion
sustenance
syllable
symmetrical
sympathize
sympathy
synchronous
synonym
syphilis
systematically
tariff
temperament
temperature
temporarily
tendency
tentative
terrestrial
therefore
thirtieth
thorough
thought
thousandth
through
till
titillate
together

tonight
tournament
tourniquet
tragedy
tragically
transferred
transient
tries
truly
twelfth
twentieth
typical
tyranny
unanimous
undoubtedly
unique
unison
unmanageable
unnecessary
until
upholsterer
usable
usage
using
usually
utilize
vacancy
vacuum
vague
valuable
variety
vegetable
veil

vengeance
vermilion
veterinarian
vichyssoise
village
villain
warrant
Wednesday
weird
wherever
whim
wholly
whose

wield
woolen
wretched
writing
written
wrote
wrought
xylophone
yacht
yield
zealous
zucchini

USING A SPELL CHECKER

A spell checker is a computer program that checks or verifies the spelling of words in an electronic document. While it can be a valuable tool for writers, it cannot be relied upon to catch all types of spelling errors. It is most useful in finding misspellings that produce "nonwords"—words with transposed, wrong, or missing letters. For example, it will reject *ther* (for *there*) and *teh* (for *the*). However, it cannot distinguish between words that sound or look alike but differ in meaning. It will accept *to* or *too* regardless of whether the context is correct, and it will accept typos such as *on* (for *of*) or *form* (for *from*). It is important, therefore, not to rely too heavily on spell checkers and to go over your writing carefully to avoid such mistakes.

RULES OF WORD DIVISION

It is often necessary to divide a word at the end of a line. Words must always be divided between syllables. Consult a dictionary if you are not sure where the syllable division occurs. The following rules should be followed to avoid confusing the reader.

1. Do not divide a one-syllable word. This includes past tenses like *walked* and *dreamed*, which should never be split before the *-ed* ending.

2. Do not divide a word so that a single letter is left at the end of a line, as in *a-bout*, or so that a single letter starts the following line, as in *cit-y*.

3. Hyphenated compounds should preferably be divided only after the hyphen. If the first portion of the compound is a single letter, however, as in *D-day*, the word should not be divided.

4. Word segments like *-ceous, -scious, -sial, -tion, -tious* should not be divided.

5. The portion of a word left at the end of a line should not encourage a misleading pronunciation, as would be the case if *acetate*, a three-syllable word, were divided after the first *e*.

Punctuation

[.] PERIOD

A *period* is used:

after a statement,

Some of us still support the mayor.

Others think he should retire.

after an indirect question,

She asked what time the train leaves.

after a mild command,

Would you close the door, please.

Read the next two chapters by Tuesday.

and after a question used as a statement.

It's hot today, isn't it.

A period is used after many abbreviations.

i.e., e.g., etc., Mr., Mrs., Ms., Dr., Inc., U.S., M.D., Sept., Pa., D.C.

A period is *not* used in acronyms, in U.S. Postal Service state abbreviations, with initials used in place of personal names, or after metric abbreviations.

UNICEF, UNESCO, NASA, NATO, IRA, AIDS, OPEC, NAFTA

NY, PA, CA, ME, MD

FDR, JFK, LBJ

50 km, 3 kg, 100 mm

A period is used within decimal numbers and amounts of money.

A sales tax of 7.5 percent is leveled on all clothing in this state.

He spent $44.50 on the shirt, $36.09 on the pants, and $22.00 on the tie.

[?] QUESTION MARK

Sentences that ask a question should be followed by a *question mark*.

Who invited him to the party?

"Is something the matter?" she asked.

What constitutional principle did John Marshall establish in *Marbury v. Madison*? in *McCullough v. Maryland*? in *Fletcher v. Peck*?

You can get us in free?

A question mark is also used to indicate doubt about information.

Socrates was born in 470 (?) B.C.E.

The code dates back to A.D. 500 (?).

A question mark is *not* used after an indirect question or after a polite command phrased as a question.

I wonder why.

She asked if the application had been mailed.

Won't you sit down.

Why don't you take off your coat.

[!] EXCLAMATION POINT

An *exclamation point* is used to end a sentence, clause, phrase, or single word that expresses a command or a strong emotion, such as surprise or admiration.

Go away!

What a week this has been!

Note: Avoid overusing exclamation points in writing. They are effective only when used sparingly.

[,] COMMA

The *comma* is the most frequently used mark of punctuation within a sentence. The main use of a comma is to clarify the structure and meaning of a sentence. The secondary use of a comma is to indicate emphasis, pauses, and stress. Adding unnecessary commas or omitting necessary ones can confuse a reader and obscure the meaning of a sentence.

Independent clauses may be grouped into sentences by using the coordinating conjunctions *and*, *but*, *yet*, *for*, *or*, *nor*, and *so*. The first clause is usually followed by a comma. If the subject of both clauses is the same, the comma is generally omitted.

We tried to reason with him, but he had already made up his mind.

Joe is finishing high school this year, and Jennifer is a junior at Harvard.

Take six cooking apples and put them into a flameproof dish.

Introductory words, phrases, clauses, and transitional expressions are set off by a comma.

Your honor, I object.

Theoretically, she will have to get the permission of the chairman.

Thoroughly chilled, he decided to set out for home.

Yes, we are prepared for any motion that the prosecution may make.

However, it is important to understand everyone's point of view.

Born to wealthy parents, he was able to pursue his career without financial worries.

After the first few years of marriage, most couples realize that there are certain matters upon which they will never agree.

Since the team was in last place, it was not surprising that only fifteen hundred fans showed up for the final game of the season.

When the introductory phrase is short, the comma is often omitted. Be certain that the sentence is clear as it stands.

In this article I will demonstrate that we have chosen the wrong policy.

At the present time the number of cigarette smokers is declining.

Conjunctive adverbs, transitional expressions, and parenthetical expressions that occur in the middle of the sentence require two commas to set them off.

It is important, however, to understand everyone's point of view.

Most new employees, after the first month, settle easily into the company's routine.

We can, I hope, agree on a budget for next year.

You may, if you insist, demand a retraction.

If a sentence can be read without pauses before and after the modifier, the commas may be omitted.

We can therefore conclude that the defendant is innocent of the charges.

The applicant must understand before sending in the forms that the deposit fee is not refundable.

A phrase or clause is called *restrictive* if omitting it would change the meaning of the sentence. Such a phrase or clause "restricts" or limits the meaning of the word or words it applies to, and therefore cannot be omitted. Restrictive phrases and clauses are not set off by commas.

The Elizabethan composers Byrd, Gibbons, and Dowland influenced her greatly.

The novel that she wrote in 1996 won a literary award.

The only state that is in the Hawaii-Aleutian time zone is Hawaii.

The city where I live is Seattle.

When a phrase or clause is not essential to the meaning of the sentence, it is called *non-restrictive*. Such phrases and clauses are set off by commas.

She was much influenced by Elizabethan composers, especially Byrd, Gibbons, and Dowland.

Her most recent novel, written in 1996, won a literary award.

Hawaii, which is the fiftieth state, is in the Hawaii-Aleutian time zone.

Seattle, the city where I live, is close to both the sea and the mountains.

Conjunctive adverbs can be placed anywhere in a sentence depending on where you want the emphasis. They are always set off by commas.

However, it is important to understand everyone's point of view.

It is important, however, to understand everyone's point of view.

It is important to understand everyone's point of view, however.

Appositives are words that give additional information about the preceding or following word or expression. Many appositives are nonrestrictive and are thus set off from the rest of the sentence with commas. Be careful not to set off restrictive appositives, which are necessary for the meaning of the sentence.

March, the month of crocuses, can still bring snow and ice.

Mr. Case, a member of the committee, refused to comment.

His favorite author, Stephen King, entered the auditorium.

My friend Mary spoke at the convention.

The crowd fell silent as the author Stephen King entered the auditorium.

A comma is used to separate words, phrases, and clauses that are part of a series of three or more items, with a word like *and* or *or* usually occurring between the last two items.

The chief agricultural products of Denmark are butter, eggs, potatoes, beets, wheat, barley, and oats.

England, Scotland, and Wales share the island of Great Britain.

Cabbage is especially good with corned beef, game, or smoked meats.

Environmentally conscious businesses use recycled paper, photocopy on both sides of a sheet, and use ceramic cups.

Note: Some writers omit the final comma when punctuating a series, and newspapers and magazines sometimes follow this practice. Book publishers and educators, however, usually follow the practice recommended above.

In a series of adjectives, commas must be used when each adjective is considered separately, not as a modifier of other adjectives.

the beautiful, expensive dress

the happy, smiling children

the hungry, meowing cat

Do not use commas to separate adjectives that are so closely related that they appear to form a single element with the noun they modify. Adjectives that refer to the number, age, size, color, or location of the noun often fall within this category. To determine whether or not to use the comma in these instances, insert the word *and*. If *and* cannot replace the comma without creating an awkward sentence, it is safe to conclude that a comma is not necessary.

twenty happy little children

several dingy old Western mining towns

beautiful tall golden aspens

a dozen long white dresses

When dates and addresses are used in sentences, they are followed by a comma. When only the month and year are given, the comma is usually omitted.

All contributions should be sent to the recording secretary at 4232 Grand Boulevard, Silver Spring, MD 70042, as soon as possible.

She was born on Tuesday, December 20, 1901, in a log cabin near Casey Creek, Kentucky.

We took our first trip to Alaska in August 1988.

Use a comma when it is necessary to prevent misreading. The comma tells the reader to stop briefly before reading on. Words may run together in confusing ways unless you use a comma to separate them. Use a comma in such sentences even though no rule requires one.

Soon after, she quit the job for good.

The people who can, usually contribute some money to the local holiday drive.

After she ate, the cat washed herself and went to sleep.

[;] SEMICOLON

A *semicolon* is used to separate parts of a sentence—such as independent clauses, items in a series, and explanations or summaries—from the main clause. It makes a stronger break in the sentence than a comma does. In choosing among the three punctuation marks that separate main clauses—the comma, the semicolon, and the colon—a writer needs to decide on the relationship between ideas.

Separate independent clauses not joined by a coordinating conjunction are separated by a semicolon.

The house burned down; it was the last shattering blow.

We have made several attempts to reach you by telephone; not a single call has been returned.

When separate independent clauses are joined by a conjunctive adverb such as *however, nevertheless, otherwise, therefore, besides, hence, indeed, instead, nonetheless, still, then,* or *thus,* a semicolon is used after the first clause.

The funds are inadequate; therefore, the project will close down.

Enrollments exceed all expectations; however, there is a teacher shortage.

He knew that tickets for the performance would be scarce; therefore, he arrived at the concert hall two hours early.

Long or possibly ambiguous items in a series, especially when those items already include commas, are separated by a semicolon.

In the next year, they plan to open stores in Sewickley, Pennsylvania; Belleville, Illinois; Breckenridge, Colorado; and Martinez, California.

Academically talented students were selected on the basis of grades; tests of vocabulary, memory, reading, inductive reasoning, math, and perceptual speed and accuracy; and teacher recommendations.

A semicolon is used before *i.e., e.g., that is, for example,* etc., when the next part of the sentence is a complete clause.

On the advice of his broker, he chose to invest in major industries; i.e., he invested in steel, automobiles, and oil.

She organizes her work well; for example, she puts correspondence in folders of different colors to indicate degrees of urgency.

[:] COLON

As a mark of introduction, the *colon* tells the reader that the first statement is going to be explained by the second or that a quotation or series will follow.

A colon is used to introduce a long formal statement or a quotation.

> This I believe: All people are created equal and must enjoy equally the rights that are inalienably theirs.

> Fagles's translation of the *Iliad* begins: "Rage—Goddess, sing the rage of Peleus' son Achilles, murderous, doomed, that cost the Achaeans countless losses, . . ."

When one independent clause is followed by another that explains or exemplifies it, they can be separated by a colon. The second clause may or may not begin with a capital letter.

> They cannot pay their monthly bills because their money is tied up in their stocks and bonds: they are paper-rich and cash-poor.

> There's only one solution: we must reduce next year's budget.

> The negotiators finally agreed on a basic principle: neither side would seek to resupply the troops during the cease-fire.

> The conference addresses a basic question: How can we take the steps needed to

protect the environment without stalling economic growth?

A colon is used to introduce a series or list.

There were originally five Marx brothers: Groucho, Chico, Harpo, Zeppo, and Gummo.

The senior citizens demanded the following: better police protection, more convenient medical facilities, and a new recreational center.

A colon is used to follow the salutation in a formal letter.

Dear Mr. Guerro:

Dear Ms. McFadden:

Dear Valued Customer:

The parts of a citation are separated by a colon.

Genesis 3:2

Journal of Astrophysics 43:2

A colon is placed between the title and the subtitle of a book.

In 1988 Brooks published *Gilded Twilight: The Later Years of Melville and Twain*.

A colon is used to separate hours from minutes in indicating time.

1:30 P.M.

12:30 A.M.

In a bibliographical citation, a colon may separate the place of publication from the name of the publisher.

New York: Random House, Inc.

Do not use a colon to introduce a list that is the object of the verb.

> The senior citizens' demands included better police protection, more convenient medical facilities, and a new recreational center.

Do not use a colon to introduce a list after the verb *to be* or to introduce a list following a preposition:

> The courses she is taking are French, medieval history, Greek, and the nineteenth-century novel.

> I have had enough of mosquitoes, leaking tents, wet blankets, and whining children.

> The committee consisted of nine teachers, twelve parents, and six business leaders.

[—] DASH

A *dash* is used to show sudden changes in thought or to set off certain sentence elements. Like the exclamation point, dashes are dramatic and thus should be used sparingly in formal writing. Do not confuse the dash with the hyphen (see page 260 on the hyphen).

The dash may be used to mark an abrupt change in thought or shift in tone.

> He won the game—but I'm getting ahead of the story.

> She told me—does she really mean it?—that she will inform us of any changes in advance.

Where commas might cause confusion, a dash may be used to set off appositives.

The premier's promise of changes—land reform and higher wages—was not easily fulfilled.

The qualities Renoir valued in his painting—rich shadows, muted colors, graceful figures—were abundant in the ballet dancers he used as subjects.

A dash may be used to add emphasis to parenthetical material or to mark an emphatic separation between that material and the rest of the sentence.

Her influence—she was a powerful figure in the community—was a deterrent to effective opposition.

The car he was driving—a gleaming red convertible—was the most impressive thing about him.

Halting or hesitant speech may be indicated by a dash.

"Well—er—it's hard to explain," he faltered.

Madame de Vionnett instantly rallied.

"And you know—though it might occur to one—it isn't in the least that he's ashamed of her.

She's really—in a way—extremely good looking."

—Henry James

Interrupted speech may also be indicated by a dash.

"Harvey, don't climb up that—." It was too late.

If they discovered the truth—he did not want to think of the consequences.

A dash may replace an offensive word or part of one.

"You're full of —!" he shouted.

Where's that son of a b—?

[...] ELLIPSIS

The *ellipsis* mark consists of three spaced periods (. . .).

It is sometimes convenient to omit part of a quotation. When this is done, the omission must be marked with points of ellipsis, usually with spaces between them. When the omission comes in the middle of a sentence, three points are used. When the omission includes the end of one or more sentences, four points are used.

Lewis Thomas offers the following advice: If something is to be quoted, the exact words must be used. If part of it must be left out . . . insert three dots to indicate the omission, but it is unethical to do this if it means connecting two thoughts which the original author did not intend to have tied together.

Ellipsis may also be used to indicate breaks in thought in quoted speech (compare with **dash**).

"I don't know where he is. . . ."

"If only she hadn't died so soon. . . ."

Note: If the sentence is complete, the period is added, resulting in four spaced periods. If the sentence is incomplete, use only three dots for the ellipsis.

[( )] PARENTHESES

Parentheses are used to enclose nonessential material within a sentence. This can include facts, explanations, digressions, and examples that may be helpful but are not necessary for the sentence. Do not put a comma before a parenthesis.

Faulkner's stories (but not his novels) were required reading for the course.

The community didn't feel (and why should they?) that there was adequate police protection.

Many workers (including those in the mail room) distrust the new shipping regulations.

Parentheses are also used to enclose part of a sentence that would be confusing if enclosed by commas.

The authors he advised (none other than Hemingway, Lewis, and Cather) would have been delighted to honor him today.

An explanatory item that is not part of the statement is enclosed in parentheses.

He wrote to *The Paris* (Illinois) *News.*

Parentheses are used to enclose numbers or letters that designate each item in a series.

The project is (1) too time-consuming, (2) too expensive, and (3) poorly staffed.

Parentheses are used to indicate an abbreviation that will be used in the remainder of the paragraph.

The Federal Trade Commission (FTC) has issued regulations on the advertising of many products.

If a full sentence is enclosed within the parentheses, the period comes before the closing parenthesis.

Seven U.S. presidents were born in Virginia. (The other southern states were the birthplaces of only one or two presidents each.) Ohio also produced seven, and Massachusetts and New York, four each.

If the parenthetical element is a fragment of a sentence, the period goes outside the closing parenthesis.

Two U.S. presidents were born in Vermont (Chester Alan Arthur and Calvin Coolidge), and one was born in New Hampshire (Franklin Pierce).

[[ ]] BRACKETS

When writers insert something within a quoted passage, the insertion should be set off with *brackets*. Insertions are sometimes used to supply words that explain, clarify, or correct the contents of a direct quotation.

According to the *Globe* critic, "This [*Man and Superman*] is one of Shaw's greatest plays."

"Young as they are," he writes, "these students are afflicted with cynicism, world-weariness, and a *total disregard for tradition and authority*." [Emphasis is mine.]

"As a result of the Gemini V mission [the flight by astronauts Cooper and Conrad in August 1965], we have proof that human beings can withstand the eight days in space required for a round trip to the moon."

Lewis Thomas warns that it is "unethical to [omit words in a quotation] . . . if it means connecting two thoughts which the original author did not intend to have tied together."

Writers can make clear that an error in the quotation has been carried over from the original by using the Latin word *sic*, meaning "thus."

"George Washington lived during the seventeenth [*sic*] century."

"The governor of Missisipi [*sic*] addressed the student body."

Brackets are used to enclose comments made in a verbatim transcript.

Sen. Eaton: The steady rise in taxes must be halted. [Applause]

Brackets are used to substitute for parentheses with material already enclosed in parentheses.

[1]See "Rene Descartes" (M.C. Beardsley, *The European Philosophers from Descartes to Nietzsche* [New York, 1960]).

The publication date, inserted by the editor, of an item appearing in an earlier issue of a periodical is enclosed in brackets.

Dear Sir: Your excellent article on China [April 15] brings to mind my recent experience . . .

When traveling in India [*Travel Monthly*, March 2001], one should recall the words of . . .

["" ""] QUOTATION MARKS

The main function of *quotation marks* is to enclose a direct quotation. Quotation marks are always used in pairs to mark the beginning and end of the quotation.

"They've come back!" she exclaimed.

Words or groups of words that are quoted from the original are enclosed in quotation marks.

Portia's speech on "the quality of mercy" is one of the most quoted passages from Shakespeare.

It was Shaw who wrote: "All great truths begin as blasphemies."

Titles of essays, short stories, poems, chapters of books, and songs are usually enclosed in quotation marks. (See the section on the use of **italics** on page 255.)

Our anthology contains such widely assorted pieces as Bacon's essay "Of Studies," Shelley's "Ode to the West Wind," Gilman's "The Yellow Wallpaper," and an article on criticism from the *New Yorker*.

"Summertime" is from *Porgy and Bess*.

Quotation marks are used to suggest that a word or phrase is being used ironically.

The radio blasting Kim's favorite "music" is to her parents an instrument of torture.

Bob's skiing "vacation" consisted of three weeks with his leg in a cast.

A quotation within a quotation is enclosed in single quotation marks.

Reading Jill's letter, Pat said, "Listen to this! 'I've just received notice that I made the dean's list.' Isn't that great?"

Final quotation marks follow other punctuation marks, except for semicolons and colons.

After dinner Ed began looking up all the unfamiliar allusions in Milton's "L'Allegro"; then, shortly after midnight, he turned to "Il Penseroso."

Question marks and exclamation marks precede final quotation marks when they refer to the quoted words. They follow when they refer to the sentence as a whole.

Once more she asked, "What do you think we should do about this?"

What do you suppose Carla meant when she said, "I'm going to do something about this"?

"Be off with you!" he yelled.

Note: Use a comma between the quotation and phrases such as *according to the speaker*, *he said*, and *she replied* that introduce or conclude a quotation.

If a quotation consists of two or more consecutive paragraphs, use quotation marks at the beginning of each paragraph, but place them at the end of the last paragraph only.

ITALICS/UNDERLINING

Italics are used to emphasize or set apart specific words and phrases. In handwritten papers, underlining indicates italics.

The titles of newspapers, magazines, and books are italicized.

> Her job requires her to read the *New York Times*, the *Wall Street Journal*, and the *Washington Post* every day.

> "Song of Myself" is the first poem in Whitman's *Leaves of Grass*.

> Every year *Consumer Reports* runs "Best Buy Gifts" in the November issue.

Italics are used for the titles of plays and movies, radio and television programs, and for the titles of works of art and long musical works.

> Shakespeare's *Hamlet*

> *The Playboy of the Western World*

> the movie *High Noon*

Huston's *The Maltese Falcon*

Leonardo da Vinci's *Last Supper*

Sesame Street

Handel's *Messiah*

Don Giovanni by Mozart

Porgy and Bess

Italics are used for the names of ships and planes.

the aircraft carrier *Intrepid*

Lindbergh's *The Spirit of St. Louis*

Words and phrases from a foreign language are italicized. Accompanying translations are often enclosed in quotation marks. Words of foreign origin that have become familiar in an English context should not be italicized.

As a group, these artists appear to be in the avant-garde. They are not, however, to be thought of as *enfants terribles*, or "terrible children," people whose work is so outrageous as to shock or embarrass.

Italics are used for words used as words and letters used as letters.

I can never remember how to spell *broccoli*.

Be sure to pronounce the final *e* in *Nike*.

Italics are used to show that words are to be emphasized.

The boss is *very* hard to get along with today.

Joan loaned the tape to Robert, and *he* gave it to Sally.

[/] FORWARD SLASH

(ALSO CALLED "SOLIDUS" OR "VIRGULE")

A *forward slash* is used to separate lines of poetry within the text.

> William Blake's stanza on anger in "A Poison Tree" seems as appropriate today as when it was first written: "I was angry with my friend: / I told my wrath, my wrath did end. / I was angry with my foe: / I told it not, my wrath did grow."

A forward slash is used in dates and fractions.

> winter 1998/99
>
> the fiscal year 2000/01
>
> 3/4 + 2/3
>
> *x/y - y/x*

Options and alternatives are separated by a forward slash.

> I have never seen the advantage of pass/fail courses.

['] APOSTROPHE

An *apostrophe* is used in contractions to show where letters or numerals have been omitted.

> I'm
>
> he's
>
> didn't
>
> won't

let's

Ma'am

four o'clock

readin', 'ritin', an' 'rithmetic

the class of '99

An apostrophe is used when making letters or numbers plural.

GI's

V.I.P.'s

figure 8's

The handwriting is very hard to read: the *n*'s and *u*'s look alike.

The number of Ph.D.'s awarded to U.S. citizens declined in the 1980's.

Note: The apostrophe may be omitted in dates: 1980s.

The apostrophe is used with nouns to show possession.

The company's management resisted the union's demands.

An apostrophe plus *s* is added to all words— singular or plural—that do not end in *-s* to show possession.

the little boy's hat

the front office's idea

children's literature

a week's vacation

somebody else's fault

the mice's tails

Just an apostrophe is added at the end of plural words that end in -*s* to show possession.

the little boys' hats

the farmers' demands

the Joneses' yard

two weeks' vacation

the oil companies' profits

for old times' sake

Style guides disagree on how to treat singular nouns that end in -*s*. Perhaps the best practice is to follow your own pronunciation. If the possessive form has an extra syllable, then add an apostrophe and *s*; otherwise just add an apostrophe.

Tess's bad luck

Socrates' worldview

for goodness' sake

Williams's poems

Dickens' (or Dickens's) novels

the class's attitude

Ulysses' voyage

Marx's philosophy

The possessive of compound words or two or more proper names is formed by adding an apostrophe plus *s* to the last word of the compound.

sister-in-law's job

editor-in-chief's pen

Japan and Germany's agreement

Lewis and Clark's expedition

the University of South Carolina's mascot

one another's books

anyone else's property

Note: Never use an apostrophe with a possessive personal pronoun. These personal pronouns are already possessive and therefore have no need for an apostrophe: *my, mine, your, yours, her, hers, its, our, ours, their,* and *theirs.*

[-] HYPHEN

Although a *hyphen* and a dash may appear to be the same at first glance, they are two very different marks of punctuation. The dash is more than twice as long as the hyphen. The hyphen is used to group words and parts of words together, while the dash is used to clarify sentence structure. A dash is formed by typing two successive hyphens (--) on a word processor that does not have a dash character.

A hyphen is used at the end of a line of text when part of a word must be carried over to the next line.

. . . insta-
bility

Hyphens are sometimes used to form compound words.

twenty-five

three-fourths

forty-one sixty-fourths

mother-in-law

president-elect

double-breasted

self-confidence

ex-wife

hands-on

the nineteen-eighties

In certain situations, hyphens are used between prefixes and root words to prevent confusion in pronunciation or to avoid confusing a word with another whose spelling is identical. If you are uncertain about a particular word, consult a dictionary.

catlike vs. bull-like

antibiotic vs. anti-intellectual

semiliterate vs. semi-invalid

recover vs. re-cover

coop vs. co-op

recreation vs. re-creation

When the root word of a compound is a proper noun or proper adjective, a hyphen is used to separate the prefix.

anti-American

neo-Nazi

non-European

pro-French

Hyphens are used to combine the elements of a compound modifier when used before the noun it modifies.

hand-to-hand combat

a well-dressed woman

a double-parked car

an out-of-work actor

an up-to-date dictionary

These modifiers are usually not hyphenated when they follow the noun, unless the compound is so common that it has become fixed.

They fought hand to hand.

She is always very well dressed.

The car was double parked.

She is out of work.

The dictionary is up-to-date.

When two modifiers are joined together, common elements are often not repeated.

This textbook covers both macro- and microeconomics.

The study included fourth-, eighth-, and twelfth-grade students.

The hyphen can be used as a substitute for *to*, with the meaning "up to and including." It should not, however, be used in conjunction with *from*.

The text of the Constitution can be found on pages 679-87.

The period 1890-1914 was a particularly tranquil time
in Europe.

The Civil War lasted from 1861 to 1865. (not *from
1861-1865*)

The San Francisco-Vancouver flight has been cancelled.

CAPITALIZATION

The important words in titles are *capitalized*. This includes the first and last words and all other words except articles, prepositions, and coordinating conjunctions, such as *and, but,* and *or*. The second element of a hyphenated compound is also not capitalized unless it is a proper noun or adjective.

Gone with the Wind

With Malice toward None

The Universe Within

Sports-related Injuries

The Brain: A User's Manual

A World to Lose

The Great War, 1914-1918

Twentieth-Century Views

Proper nouns—names of specific people, places, organizations, groups, events, etc.— are capitalized, as are the proper adjectives derived from them.

Martin Luther King, Jr.

United States Coast Guard

New Orleans

Canada

Latinos

Spanish Civil War

Canadian

Jeffersonian

When proper nouns and adjectives have taken on a specialized meaning, they are often no longer capitalized.

My brother ordered a turkey sandwich with russian dressing.

The shop specializes in china and plaster of paris ornaments.

The address was written in india ink on a manila envelope.

Titles of people are capitalized when they are used before a name or when they are used in place of a name to refer to the specific person who holds the title. They are not capitalized when they refer to the office rather than to the person.

Queen Victoria reigned from 1837 to 1901. The Queen's husband, Prince Albert, died in 1861. Some of England's greatest novels were written while she was queen.

President Lincoln was assassinated in 1865. The President and his wife were attending a performance at Ford's Theater. During the years he was president, the South seceded from the Union, and the Civil War began.

Kinship terms are capitalized when they are used before a name or alone in place of a name. They are not capitalized when they are preceded by modifiers.

I'm expecting Aunt Alice to drop by this weekend.

I forgot to call Mother on her birthday.

I forgot to call my mother on her birthday.

Geographical features are capitalized when they are part of the official name. In the plural, they are capitalized when they precede names, but not when they follow.

The Sonoran Desert is in southern Arizona.

The Arizona desert is beautiful in the spring.

In recent years, Lakes Erie and Ontario have been cleaned up.

The Hudson and Mohawk rivers are both in New York State.

Points of the compass are capitalized only when they are used as the name of a section of the country.

We've been driving east for over two hours.

We visited the South last summer and the Southwest the year before.

He was born in southwestern Nebraska.

Prefixes, Suffixes, and Roots

COMMON PREFIXES
AND THEIR MEANINGS

a- **1.** place or state (*ashore, asleep*).
2. not (*atypical*). **3.** without (*amoral*).

ab- off, away (*abnormal*).

ad- toward (*adhere, adjoin*).

ambi- both (*ambiance, ambiguous, ambivalence*).

amphi- both (*amphibian, amphibious*); on two sides (*amphitheater*).

ante- **1.** happening before (*antebellum*).
2. in front of (*anteroom*).

anti- **1.** against (*antislavery*). **2.** preventing or counteracting (*anticoagulant, antifreeze*). **3.** destroying or disabling (*antiaircraft, antipersonnel*). **4.** rival of (*Antichrist, antipope*). **5.** identical in some respects (*anticlimax, antihero, antipartical*).

aqua- water (*aquarium*).

auto- self (*autograph*).

bi- twice, two (*bicentennial, bigamy, bipartisan, bisect*).

bio- life (*biodegradable, biology*).

centi- hundred (*centipede*); hundredth (*centimeter*).

circum- round, around (*circuit, circumvent, circus*).

co- **1.** joint (*costar*). **2.** auxiliary, helping (*copilot*).

com- (or **con-**) with, together with (*combine, compare, confer, convene*).

contra- against, opposite, opposing (*contraception, contradict, contrary*).

counter- against (*counterattack, counterclockwise*).

de- **1.** motion down or away (*deplane, descend*). **2.** reversing or undoing the effects of an action (*deflate, dehumanize*). **3.** removal of something (*decaffeinate*). **4.** finishing or completeness of an action (*defunct, despoil*).

deci- ten (*decibel*).

demi- half (*demigod*).

demo- people (*democracy*).

di- two (*diptych*); double (*dioxide*).

dia- through or across (*diameter, diaphanous*); completely (*diagnosis*).

dis- **1.** opposite of (*disagreement*). **2.** not (*disapprove, dishonest, disobey*). **3.** reverse; remove (*disconnect, discontinue, dissolve*)

dys- ill, bad (*dysfunctional, dyslexia, dyspepsia*).

en-[1] **1.** to cause (person or thing) to be in (the place or state mentioned); keep or place in (*enrich, entomb*). **2.** to restrict completely (*encircle*).

en-[2] in (*enthusiasm*).

epi- 1. on, at (*epicenter*). 2. outer (*epidermis*). 3. additional (*episode*).

eu- good, well (*eulogy, euphemism, euphoria*).

ex- 1. out or out of (*exclude, exhale, exit*). 2. former (*ex-member*).

extra- outside of (*extragalactic*) or beyond (*extrasensory*).

fore- 1. before (*forecast, foretaste*). 2. front (*forehead*). 3. preceding (*forefather*). 4. superior (*foreman*).

hemo- blood (*hemoglobin*).

hyper- excessive (*hypercritical*); overly (*hypertension*).

hypo- under (*hypodermic*); below (*hypothermia*).

il-[1] (another form of **in-**[1]) in, into (*illuminate*).

il-[2] (another form of **in-**[2]) not (*illegible*).

im-[1] (another form of **in-**[1]) in, into (*immigrate*).

im-[2] (another form of **in-**[2]) not (*impossible*).

in-[1] in, into; on (*income*).

in-[2] not (*inaccurate*).

inter- between or among (*intercity, inter-collegiate*).

intra- within (*intraspecies*).

intro- inside (*introduce*).

ir-[1] (another form of **in-**[1]) in, into (*irradiate*).

ir-[2] (another form of **in-**[2]) not (*irreducible*).

kilo- thousand (*kilometer*).

mal- bad (*malfunction*).

mega- **1.** huge (*megalith*). **2.** one million (*megahertz*).

meta- after, along with, beyond, among, behind (*metabolism, metamorphosis, metaphor, metaphysics*)

micro- **1.** small (*microorganism*). **2.** restricted in scope (*microhabitat*). **3.** one millionth (*microgram*).

milli- **1.** one thousand (*millipede*). **2.** one thousandth (*millimeter*).

mis- **1.** wrong (*misprint*). **2.** the opposite of (*mistrust*).

mono- one, single (*monarch, monochrome, monocle, monotonous*).

multi- many, much (*multicolored, multivitamin*).

neo- new (*neonatal*).

neuro- nerve (*neurosurgeon*).

non- not (*nonviolent, nonpayment*).

octa- eight (*octagon*).

omni- all (*omniscient*).

ortho- straight, correct (*orthodontics*).

pan- all (*panorama, pantheism*).

para- 1. beside (*paragraph, parabola*).
2. beyond (*paradox*). 3. abnormal
(*paranoia*). 4. assisting (*paralegal*).

penta- five (*pentagon*).

per- through, completely (*perfect,
pervade*).

peri- 1. around (*perimeter, periscope*).
2. surrounding (*pericardium*). 3. near
(*perihelion*).

petro- rock (*petrology*).

photo- light (*photosynthesis*).

poly- many (*polyphony*).

post- after, behind (*postwar, postscript*).

pre- before (*predict*), in front of (*preface*),
surpassing (*preeminent*).

pro-[1] 1. forward (*proceed, promote*).
2. bringing into existence (*procreate*).
3. in place of (*pronoun*). 4. favoring
(*pro-choice*).

pro-[2] 1. before (*prognosis*), in front of
(*proboscis*). 2. early form (*prosimian*).

proto- earliest form of (*protoplasm*).

pseudo- 1. false (*pseudonym*). 2. closely
resembling (*pseudopod*).

psycho- soul, mind (*psychedelic, psychiatry,
psychology*).

pyro- fire (*pyrotechnics*).

quasi- resembling (*quasi-scientific, quasi-
particle*).

Common Prefixes and Their Meanings **273**

re- **1.** action in a backward direction (*recede*). **2.** action in answer to or reversing a situation (*respond, restore*). **3.** action that is done over (*recapture*).

retro- back, backward (*retrogress*).

semi- **1.** half (*semicircle*). **2.** partially (*semiformal*).

sex- six (*sexpartite*).

sub- **1.** under (*subway*). **2.** just outside of (*subtropical*). **3.** less than (*subhuman*). **4.** secondary (*subplot*).

super- **1.** above (*superstructure, superficial*). **2.** exceeding customary levels (*superman*).

sur- over, in addition (*surcharge*).

syn- (or **sym-**) with, together (*synchronize, symphony*).

tele- far (*telegraph, television*).

trans- across, through (*transfer, transform, trans-Siberian*).

tri- three (*trilateral*).

ultra- beyond (*ultraviolet*); extremely (*ultramodern*).

un-¹ not (*unemployment, unfair, unformed*).

un-² **1.** reversal of an action (*unfasten*). **2.** intensifying the meaning of a verb (*unloose*).

under- 1. a place beneath (*underbrush*).
2. lower in rank (*understudy*). 3. of lesser
degree (*undersized*). 4. too little (*under-fed*).

vice- in place of; deputy (*vice president*).

COMMON SUFFIXES AND THEIR MEANINGS

-able, added to verbs to form adjectives meaning "capable of, fit for, tending to" (*teachable*).

-aceous, made of (*herbaceous*).

-acious, tending to (*loquacious*).

-acity, used after roots to form nouns meaning "tendency toward" (*tenacity*).

-age, used to form noncount mass or abstract nouns **1.** from other nouns with meanings such as "collection" (*coinage*) and "quantity or measure" (*footage*). **2.** from verbs, with meanings such as "process" (*coverage*), "the outcome of or the remains of" (*spoilage; wreckage*), and "amount charged" (*towage, postage*).

-al^1, added to nouns to form adjectives meaning "relating to, having the form of" (*autumnal, natural*).

-al^2, added to verbs to form nouns meaning "the act of" (*denial*).

-an, 1. added to names or places or people to form adjectives and nouns meaning **a.** "being connected with a place" (*Chicagoan*); **b.** "having membership in a group of" (*Episcopalian*). **2.** used to form adjectives meaning "of or like (someone); "supporter of or believer in" (*Christian, Freudian*). **3.** used to form nouns from words ending in *-ic* or *-y* meaning "one who works with" (*electrician, comedian*).

-ance, quality or state of (*brillance*).

-ant, 1. used after some verbs to form adjectives meaning "doing or performing (the action of the verb)" (*pleasant*). **2.** used after some verbs to form nouns meaning "one who does or performs (the action of the verb)" (*applicant, servant*). **3.** used after verbs to form nouns meaning "substance that does or performs (the action of the verb)" (*coolant*).

-ard, used after verbs and adjectives to form nouns that refer to persons who regularly do an activity or who are characterized in a certain way (*dullard, drunkard*).

-arian, 1. used after nouns and adjectives to form personal nouns (*librarian, seminarian, veterinarian*). **2.** used after roots to form nouns meaning "a person who supports or practices the principles of" (*authoritarian, totalitarian*).

-ary, 1. used after nouns to form adjectives meaning "relating to" (*honorary*). **2.** used to form personal nouns or nouns referring to objects that contain things (*library*). **3.** used after nouns to form adjectives meaning "contributing to or for the purpose of" (*inflationary, complimentary*).

-ate, 1. full of (*passionate*). **2.** cause to become (*activate*). **3. a.** group of people (*electorate*). **b.** area ruled by (*protectorate*). **c.** office of (*consulate*).

-ation, state or process of (*starvation*).

-ator, person or thing that does the action indicated by the verb (*agitator*).

-cracy, used after roots to form nouns meaning "rule, government" (*democracy*).

-crat, used after roots to form nouns meaning "ruler, member of a ruling body" (*autocrat*).

-cy, 1. used to form abstract nouns (*accuracy*) or action nouns (*vacancy*). 2. used to form nouns meaning "office of" (*captaincy*).

-dom, 1. area ruled (*kingdom*). 2. collection of persons (*officialdom*). 3. rank (*earldom*). 4. general condition (*freedom*).

-ee, 1. used to form nouns indicating the person who is the object of the action of the verb (*addressee*). 2. used to form nouns indicating the one doing the act of the verb (*escapee*). 3. used to form nouns indicating the one who is or does (*absentee*).

-en, 1. a. be or make (*harden*). b. cause to be or have (*lengthen*). 2. used to form adjectives that describe material (*golden*).

-ence, quality or state of (*abstinence*).

-ent, 1. doing or performing (*different*). 2. one who does something (*student*).

-ery (or **-ry**), used to form nouns referring to things or people as a group (*greenery,* *peasantry*) or to an occupation or condition (*dentistry, rivalry*) or to a place where an activity takes place (*bakery*).

-ese, 1. used after nouns that refer to place names: **a.** to form adjectives to describe things made in or relating to the place (*Japanese, Viennese*). **b.** to form nouns that describe in an insulting or humorous way the language characteristic of the base word (*Brooklynese, journalese*).

-esque, in the style or manner of (*Kafka-esque, Lincolnesque*).

-fest, an assembly of people engaged in a common activity (*songfest*).

-fold, having the number of kinds or parts or multiplied the number of times (*fourfold, manyfold*).

-ful, 1. used after nouns to form adjectives meaning "full of or characterized by" (*beautiful, careful*). **2.** used after verbs to form adjectives meaning "tending to" (*harmful, wakeful*). **3.** used after nouns to form nouns meaning "as much as will fill" (*cupful, spoonful*).

-fy, 1. used to form verbs meaning "to make" (*purify, simplify*). **2.** used to form verbs meaning "to cause to conform to" (*citify*).

-gon, side, angle (*polygon*).

-gram, something written or drawn (*epigram, diagram*).

-graph, written down or drawn (*homograph, photograph*).

-hearted, used after adjectives to form adjectives meaning "having the character or personality of" (*coldhearted, light-hearted*)

-hood, 1. the state or condition of (*likelihood, childhood*). **2.** a group of persons of a particular class (*priesthood*).

-iatrics (or **-iatry**)**,** the medical practice of (*geriatrics, pediatrics, podiatry, psychiatry*).

-ible, capable of, tending to (*credible, reducible*).

-ic, used after nouns to form adjectives meaning "of or relating to or having the characteristics of" (*metallic, Byronic*).

-ics, used after roots to form nouns meaning "body of knowledge or principles" (*ethics, physics*).

-ier, used after nouns or roots to form nouns meaning "person or thing that does something" (*financier*) or "person that is in charge of something" (*hotelier*).

-ine, used after roots or nouns to form adjectives meaning "of, relating to, or characteristic of" (*equine*) or "made of" (*crystalline*).

-ion, used to form nouns that refer to action or condition (*union*).

-ish, 1. used to form adjectives meaning a. "relating to; in the same manner of;

having the characteristics of" (*brutish*).
b. "of or relating to the people or language of" (*British, Swedish*). **c.** "like, similar to" (*babyish, girlish*). **d.** "addicted to; inclined to" (*bookish*). **e.** "near or about" (*fiftyish*). **2.** used after adjectives to form adjectives meaning "somewhat, rather" (*oldish, reddish*).

-ism, 1. used after verb roots to form nouns (*baptism*). **2.** used to form nouns showing action or practice (*adventurism*). **3.** used to form nouns showing state or condition (*alcoholism*). **4.** used after roots to form nouns showing the names of principles or doctrines (*Darwinism, despotism*). **5.** used to form nouns showing an example of a use (*witticism, Americanism*).

-ist, used to form nouns referring to a person who practices or is concerned with something (*novelist, terrorist*).

-ite, 1. used to form nouns meaning a person associated with a place or a set of beliefs (*Manhattanite, Laborite*). **2.** used to form nouns meaning mineral or fossil; explosive; chemical compound or drug product (*anthracite, dynamite, sulfite*).

-itis, used after roots that refer to an inflammation or disease affecting a certain part of the body (*appendicitis, bronchitis*).

-ive, used to form adjectives meaning "having a tendency or connection with" (*active, sportive*).

-ize, 1. used to form verbs meaning "to cause to become" (*sterilize*). **2.** used to form verbs meaning "to change to a state of" (*dramatize*). **3.** used to form verbs meaning "to subject to" (*hospitalize*).

-less, 1. without (*careless, shameless*). **2.** that cannot be (*countless*).

-let, 1. used after a noun to form a noun that is a smaller version of the original (*booklet*). **2.** used after a noun to form a noun that is a band or ornament worn on the part of the body mentioned (*anklet*).

-ling, 1. used to form a noun that indicates a feeling of distaste for the person or thing named (*hireling*). **2.** used to form a noun that is a smaller version of the base word (*duckling*).

-logy, used after roots to form nouns meaning "field of study or discipline" (*anthropology, biology*).

-ly, 1. used after adjectives to form adverbs (*gladly, gradually*). 2. used after nouns that refer to units or time, to form adjectives and adverbs meaning "at or for every (such unit of time)" (*daily, hourly*). **3.** used after nouns to form adjectives meaning "like (the noun mentioned)" (*saintly, cowardly*).

-mania, used after roots to form nouns meaning "enthusiasm, often extreme" (*bibliomania*).

282 *Common Suffixes and Their Meanings*

-ment, 1. used after verbs to form nouns that refer to the action of the verb (*government*). **2.** used after verbs to form nouns that refer to a state or condition resulting from the action of a verb (*refreshment*). **3.** used after verbs to form nouns that refer to a product resulting from the action of a verb (*fragment*).

-ness, used after adjectives and verbs to form nouns that refer to the quality or state of the adjective or verb (*darkness, preparedness*).

-off, used to form nouns that name or refer to a competition or contest (*cookoff, runoff*).

-oid, used to form adjectives and nouns meaning "resembling or like," with the suggestion of an imperfect similarity to the root element (*factoid, humanoid*).

-onym, word, name (*homonym, pseudonym*).

-or, used to form nouns that do or perform a function (*debtor, projector, sensor, traitor*).

-ory[1], 1. of or relating to (*sensory*). **2.** providing (*satisfactory*).

-ory[2], used to form nouns referring to places or things that are used for something (*crematory, observatory*).

-ose, used to form adjectives meaning "full of" (*verbose*) or "tending to" (*bellicose*).

-ous, used to form adjectives meaning "possessing of full of" (*glorious, wondrous*).

-phile, used to form nouns meaning "lover of, enthusiast for" (*Francophile, bibliophile*).

-phobe, used to from nouns that refer to persons who have a fear of something named by the root or preceding word (*Anglophobe*).

-phobia, used to form nouns meaning "dread or fear of " (*agoraphobia, xenophobia*).

-phobic, used to form adjectives or nouns meaning "(a person) having a continuous, irrational fear or hatred toward" the object named (*xenophobic*).

-ship, **1.** state or quality (*friendship*). **2.** position or rank (*lordship*). **3.** skill or art (*horsemanship*).

-some¹, like (*burdensome*) or tending to (*quarrelsome*).

-some², collection of objects (*threesome*).

-ster, used to form nouns, often implying a bad or negative sense, and referring esp. to one's occupation, habit, or association (*gamester, trickster*).

-tion, used to form nouns that refer to actions or states (*relation, abbreviation*).

-tious, used after roots to form adjectives (*fictitious, ambitious, cautious*).

-tude, used to form nouns that refer to abstract ideas (*exactitude*).

-ty, used to form nouns that refer to state or condition (*ability*).

-ure, used to form abstract nouns that refer to action, result, instrument, or use (*legislature, fracture*).

-ville, 1. city or town (*Charlottesville*). **2.** used after roots or words to form informal words that characterize a condition, place, person, group, or situation (*dullsville, gloomsville*).

-ward, used to form adjectives or adverbs meaning "toward a certain direction in space or time" (*backward*).

-ways, used to form adjectives or adverbs meaning "in a certain direction, manner, or position" (*sideways*).

-wide, 1. used to form adjectives and adverbs meaning "extending through a certain space" (*worldwide*).

-wise, 1. used to form adjectives and adverbs meaning "in a particular manner or direction" (*clockwise*). **2.** used to form adverbs meaning "with reference to" (*timewise*).

-worthy, 1. used to form adjectives meaning "deserving of " (*newsworthy*). 2. used to form adjectives meaning "capable of travel in or on" (*seaworthy*).

COMMON ROOTS AND THEIR MEANINGS

-acr- sharp (*acerbic, acrid*).

-acro- high (*acrobat, acrophobia*).

-act- do, move (*action, transact*).

-ag- move (*agitate*); do (*agent*).

-agon- struggle (*agony, antagonist*).

-agr- farming, field (*agriculture, agronomy*).

-alg- pain (*analgesic, neuralgia*).

-ali- other, different (*alias, alien*).

-alte- other, different (*alternate, alternative*).

-alti- high, height (*altitude, exalt*).

-am- like, love (*amiable, paramour*).

-ambl- walk (*amble, ambulatory*).

-ampl- enough (*ample*), enlarge, (*amplify*).

-andro- male, man (*androgynous, android*).

-anima- spirit, soul (*animate, equanimity*).

-ann- year (*annual, anniversary*).

-anthro- human (*anthropocentric, anthropology*).

-apt- fit, proper (*adapt, aptitude*).

-arch- 1. leader, ruler (*archbishop, matriarch, anarchy, monarchy*). 2. first, original (*archaeology, archaic, archetype*). 3. used to form nouns that refer to persons who are the most notable or most extreme examples of the following noun (*archconservative, archenemy*).

-arm- weapon (*armada, armament*).

-astro- (or **-aster-**) star (*asterisk, astronomy*).

-athl- contest (*athletic, pentathlon*).

-aud- hear (*audible, auditorium*).

-bat- beat, fight (*battle, combat*).

-bell- war (*antebellum, belligerent*).

-bene- well (*benediction, benefit*).

-biblio- book (*bibliography, bible*).

-brev- short (*abbreviate, brief*).

-cap- take, hold (*capture, caption*).

-caut- care, careful (*caution, cautious*).

-cede- (or **-ceed-** or **-cess-**) go, yield (*accede, proceed, succession*).

-ceive- get (*conceive, receive*).

-celer- quick (*accelerate, celerity*).

-cent- one hundred (*century, centigrade*).

-cep- get, receive, take (*accept, perception*).

-cert- sure, true (*certain, certificate*).

-chor- sing (*choir, choral, chord*); dance (*choreograph*).

-chrom- color (*chromatic, monochrome*).

-chron- time (*chronic, chronology*).

-cide-[1] kill (*genocide, homicide*).

-cide-[2] fall, happen (*accident, incident*).

-cise- cut (*incision, scissors*).

-claim- call out (*exclaim, clamor*).

-clos- close (*cloister, closet*).

-clud- (or **-clus-**) close, shut (*include, seclusion*).

-cord- heart (*concord, cordial*).

-corp- body (*corporal, corpse*).

-cosmo- universe (*cosmic*), world (*cosmopolitan*).

-cred- believe (*credential, creed, incredible*).

-cres- grow (*crescendo, decrease*).

-culp- blame (*culpable, culprit*).

-cur- (or -**cour-**) run (*current, courier, curriculum, occur*).

-cura- care (*accurate, curator*).

-cycle- circle (*bicycle, cyclotron*).

-dent- tooth (*dentist, denture*).

-derm- skin (*dermatology, hypodermic*).

-dict- say, speak (*benediction, contradict, dictionary, dictator, predict*).

-doc- teach (*doctor, doctrine, document*).

-dox- belief (*doxology, orthodox*).

-du- two (*duel, duplex, duplicity*).

-duc- lead (*abduct, induce, introduce, produce, reduce, seduce*).

-dur- hard (*durable, endure*).

-dyn- power (*dynamic, dynamite, dynasty*).

-equa- (or **-equi-**) equal; the same (*equilibrium, equivocal, inequity*).

-fac- (or **-fic-** or **-fec-**) do, make (*facsimile, manufacture, fiction, prolific, affect, infect*).

-face- face (*deface, facade*).

-fed- group, league (*confederate, federal*).

-fend- strike (*defend, offend*).

-fer- carry (*differ, transfer*).

-fess- declare; acknowledge (*confess, profession*).

-fid- faith, trust (*confidence, fidelity*).

-fin- end or limit (*confine, final*).

-fix- fastened (*fixation, prefix*).

-flat- blow; wind (*deflate, flatulence*).

-flect- (or **-flex-**) bend (*deflect, genuflect, flexible*).

-flor- flower (*floral, flourish*).

-flu- flow (*affluence, fluctuate*).

-foli- leaf (*defoliate, folio*).

-form- form, shape (*conform, uniform*).

-fort- strong, strength (*comfort, fortify*).

-frac- break (*fraction, fracture*).

-frat- brother (*fraternity, fratricide*).

-fug- run or flee (*fugue, refuge*).

-fus- pour, cast (*fuse, diffuse*); mix or blend (*confuse, transfusion*).

-gam- marriage (*bigamy, gamete*).

-gen- birth, born, produced (*congenital, gender, gene*).

-geo- earth, ground (*geography, geology*).

-gest- carry, bear (*gesture, suggest*).

-glot- tongue (*epiglottis, glossary*).

-gnos- knowledge (*agnostic, recognize*).

-grad- degree (*centigrade, undergraduate*).

-graph- written down, printed, drawn (*biography, graphic*).

-grat- pleasing, thankful (*congratulate, gratuity*).

-greg- group, flock (*congregate, gregarious*).

-gress- step, move (*congress, progress*).

-gyn- wife, woman (*gynecology, misogyny*).

-hab- live, reside (*habitat, inhabit*).

-habil- handy; able (*ability, rehabilitate*).

-hale- breathe (*exhale, halitosis*).

-hap- luck, chance (*haphazard, perhaps*).

-helio- sun (*aphelion, heliocentric*).

-here- (or **-hes-**) cling (*adhere, coherence, adhesive*).

-hetero- the other of two; different (*heterogeneous, heterosexual*).

-hexa- six (*hexagon, hexameter*).

-homo- same (*homogenize, homonym*).

-hum- ground (*exhume, humility*).

-hydr- water (*dehydration, hydrant*).

-jac- (or **-jec-**) throw or place (*adjacent, inject, project, trajectory*).

-jour- day (*journal, sojourn*).

-jud- judge (*adjudicate, prejudice*).

-junc- join, connect (*adjunct, injunction*).

-jur- swear (*abjure, jury*).

-jus- law or right (*justice, maladjusted*).

-lab- to work (*collaborate, labor*).

-lat-[1] carried (*correlate, relate*).

-lat-[2] line, side (*equilateral, latitude*).

-lax- loose, slack (*laxative, relax*).

-lec- gather, choose (*collect, elect*); read (*lectern, lecture*).

-leg- law (*legislate, paralegal, privilege*); read (*legend, legible*).

-lev- lift (*elevate*); be light (*levity*).

-liber- free (*liberal, liberty*).

-libr- book (*library, libretto*).

-libra- balance; weigh (*deliberate, equilibrium*).

-lig- tie, bind (*ligature, obligate, religion*).

-lim- line, edge, threshold (*illimitable, sublime*).

-lin- string, line (*delineate, lineage, linen, lingerie, patrilineal*).

-ling- tongue (*bilingual, linguistic*).

-lit- letter; word (*alliteration, literary*).

-lith- stone (*megalith, paleolithic*).

-loc- place (*allocate, location*).

-log- speak; word (*eulogy, logo*).

-loq- (or **-loc-**) speak; say (*soliloquy, circumlocution*).

-lu- (or **-lav-**) wash (*dilute, lavatory*).

-luc- light (*elucidate, lucubrate*).

-lud- (or **-lus-**) play or playful (*allude, ludicrous, illusion*).

-lys- break down, loosen (*analysis, hydrolysis*).

-man-[1] hand (*manual, manuscript*).

-man-[2] stay (*permanent, remain*).

-mand- order (*command, demand*).

-mater- mother (*maternal, matriarch*).

-mech- machine, tool (*machination, mechanic*).

-medi- middle (*immediate, mediator*).

-mem- mind; memory (*commemorate, memorial*).

-men- mind (*mental, mention*).

-merc- trade (*commerce, mercenary*).

-merg- (or **-mers-**) plunge or dip (*submerge, immerse*).

-meter- measure (*barometer, metric*).

-migr- move to a new place (*immigrate, migrant*).

-min- least (*diminish, miniature*).

-mis- send (*dismiss, missile*).

-misc- mix (*miscellaneous, promiscuous*).

-miser- wretched (*commiserate, miserable*).

-mit- send (*commit, submit*).

-mne- mind, remembering (*amnesty, mnemonic*).

-mob- move (*automobile, mobilize*).

-mod- manner, kind (*immodest, model*).

-mon- warn (*admonish, monitor*).

-monstr- show (*demonstrate, monstrance*).

-mor- custom (*moral, morale*).

-morph- form; shape (*amorphous, metamorphosis*).

-mort- death (*immortal, mortgage*).

-mot- (or **-mov-**) move (*automotive, removal*).

-mut- change (*commute, mutation*).

-nat- (or **-nasc-**) born, birth (*innate, nativity*).

-naut- sailor, traveler (*astronaut, nautical*).

-nav- boat, ship (*navigate, navy*).

-nec- (or **-nex-**) tie, bind (*connect, nexus*).

-neg- deny, nothing (*negative, negligible*).

-noc- (or **-nox-**) harm, kill (*innocent, noxious*).

-noct- night (*nocturnal, nocturne*).

-nom-[1] custom, law (*astronomy, economy*).

-nom-[2] name (*denomination, misnomer*).

-norm- rule, pattern (*enormous, normal*).

-nov- new (*innovation, novel*).

-null- none (*annul, nullify*).

-num- number (*enumerate, supernumerary*).

-nunc- call, say (*annunciation, enunciate*).

-ocul- eye (*binocular, monocle*).

-oper- work (*cooperate, opera, operate*).

-opt- choose (*adopt, option*).

-opti- light; sight (*autopsy, myopic, optic, optometry*).

-ord- order, fit (*extraordinary, subordinate*).

-ori- rise, begin (*orient, origin*).

-pac- peace (*pacific, pacify*).

-pact- fasten (*compact, impact*).

-par- equal (*apart, compare*)

-pare-1 prepare (*apparatus, preparation, separate*).

-pare-2 bring forth (*parent, postpartum*).

-pass- step, pace (*compass, impasse, passport*).

-pat- (or **-pass-**) suffer (*compassion, patient*).

-path- suffering, disease (*pathology, psychopath*); feeling (*empathy, pathos, telepathy*).

-patr- father (*paternal, patriot*).

-ped-1 foot (*centipede, pedestrian*).

-ped-2 child (*pedagogue, pediatrics*).

-pel- drive, push (*expel, propeller*).

-pen- wrong (*penalize, repent*).

-pend- hang (*append, independent*).

-phil- love (*philharmonic, philosophy*).

-phon- sound (*cacaphony, microphone, phonics, phonograph*).

-phys- natural science (*physician, physics*).

-plac- please (*complacent, placid*).

-plen- (or **-plet-**) full (*plenary, plenty, complete, replenish*).

-plex- fold (*complex, duplex*).

-plic- fold, bend (*complicate, explicit*).

-pod- foot (*podiatrist, tripod*).

-point- point, pierce (*appoint, midpoint*).

-poli- smooth (*polish, polite*).

-polis- city (*cosmopolitan, politics, police, policy*).

-pon- put, place (*component, postpone*).

-pop- people (*populace, popular*).

-port- carry, bring (*export, portable*).

-posit- put, place (*deposit, position*).

-pot- power (*impotent, potential*).

-preci- value (*appreicate, precious*).

-prehend- grasp (*apprehend, comprehend*).

-press- squeeze, press (*compress, depression, impressive*).

-prim- first (*primary, primate*).

-pris- grasp (*comprise, prison*).

-priv- seaparted (*deprive, private*).

-prob- prove (*improbable, probation*).

-propr- one's own (*appropriate, property*).

-prov- prove (*approve, disapprove*).

-prox- near (*approximate, proximity*).

-pter- wing (*helicopter, pterodactyl*).

-pugn- fight (*impugn, pugnacious*).

-puls- push (*expulsion, impulse*).

-punct- point, pierce (*acupuncture, punctual*).

-pur- pure (*expurgate, purge*).

-quad- four (*quadrangle, quadruplet*).

-quer- (or **-ques-**) seek (*conquer, query, quest*).

-quie- quiet, still (*acquiese, quietude*).

-quir- (or **-quis-**) seek, look for (*acquire, inquiry, inquisitive*).

-quit- release (*acquit, requite*).

-quot- how many (*quota, quotient*).

-rape- carry off by force (*enrapture, rapid, rapine*).

-rase- scrape (*abrasion, raze*).

-ratio- reason, judgment (*ratify, rational*).

-real- in fact (*reality, surreal*).

-rect- right, straight (*direct, rectangle, rectify*).

-reg- rule (*regular, regimen*).

-rend- give (*render, surrender*).

-roga- ask, demand (*arrogant, prerogative*).

-rota- round (*rotary, rotunda*).

-rupt- break (*corrupt, rupture*).

-salv- save (*salvation, salvage*).

-san- health (*insane, sanitary*).

-sanct- holy (*sanctify, sanctuary*).

-sat- full, enough (*dissatisfy, saturate*).

-scend- climb (*ascend, condescend*).

-sci- know (*omniscient, science*).

-scope- see (*microscope, telescope*).

-scrib- write (*describe, scribble*).

-script- writing (*description, scripture*).

-sect- cut (*bisect, section*).

-semble- seem, appear (*dissemble, semblance*).

-sene- old (*senate, senile*).

-sens- (or **-sent-**) sense, feel (*extrasensory, sensation, sentient*).

-seq- follow (*consequence, sequential, obsequious, sequal*).

-serv-[1] slave (*servant, servile, service*).

-serv-[2] save (*conserve, observe, reservoir*).

-sid- sit; stay (*preside, residual*).

-sign- sign; have meaning (*assign, design, insignia, signal*).

-simil- alike, similar (*assimilate, facsimile, simulate, simultaneous*).

-sist- remain, stand (*inconsistent, subsist*).

-soc- partner, comrade (*associate, society*).

-sole- alone (*soliloquy, solitary*).

-solv- loosen, release (*dissolve, resolve*).

-som- body (*chromosome, psychosomatic*).

-son- sound (*consonant, sonata*).

-soph- wise (*philosophy, sophisticated*).

-spec- look at (*inspect, perspective, spectacle, species, suspect*).

298 *Common Roots and Their Meanings*

-spir- breathe (*expire, spirit*).

-stab- stand (*establish, stable*).

-stan- stand, remain (*inconstant, distant, substantive, stanchion*).

-stat- stand, remain (*interstate, photostat, static, statue*).

-strict- draw tight (*constrict, stricture*).

-stroph- turn, twist (*apostrophe, catastrophe*).

-sum- take or pick up (*assume, presume*).

-tact- (or **-tang-**) touch (*contact, tactile, tangible*).

-tail- cut (*curtail, tailor*).

-tain- hold (*attain, maintain*).

-tech- skill (*polytechnic, technique*).

-temp- time (*contemporary, tempo*).

-ten- hold (*content, tenable*).

-tend- stretch (*tendon, extend*); proceed (*tendency*).

-term- end, limit (*determine, terminate*).

-terr- earth (*terrain, territory*).

-test- witness (*attest, testimony*).

-theo- god (*atheist, theology*).

-therm- heat (*hypothermia, thermometer*).

-tom- cut (*atom, vasectomy*).

-ton- sound (*atonal, undertone*).

-tort- twist (*distort, torture*).

-tox- poison (*intoxicated, toxic*).

Common Roots and Their Meanings **299**

-trac- pull (*attract, traction*).

-turb- stir up (*disturb, turbulent*).

-type- impression (*archetype, typical*).

-ult- beyond (*ulterior, ultimate*).

-uni- one (*reunion, unicorn, unit, unique*).

-urb- city (*suburb, urban*).

-vac- empty (*vacant, vacuum*).

-vade- go (*invade, pervade*).

-val- worth(*valor, value, validate*).

-var- change (*variable, variety*).

-ven- come (*advent, convent, covenant, event, souvenir, venture*).

-ver- true, truth (*veracity, verity*).

-verb- word (*proverb, verbose*).

-verg- turn, bend (*converge, diverge*).

-vert- (or **-vers-**) turn (*divert, adverse, vertebrate, incontrovertible, perversion*).

-via- way, route (*deviant, viaduct*).

-vict- (or **-vinc-**) conquer (*evict, victory, vincible*).

-vide- (or **-vis-**) see (*evident, video, visit, invisible, vision*).

-vit- live, alive (*revival, survivor*).

-voc- call (*evocative, revoke, vociferous*).

-vol- wish or want (*benevolent, voluntary*).

-volv- (or **-volut-**) turn, roll (*evolve, revolution*).

300 *Common Roots and Their Meanings*

-vor- eat (*carnivore, devour*).
-vot- vow (*devout, vote*).
-voy- send (*envoy, voyage*).

INDEX

Abbreviations, 235
Acronyms, 235
Action verbs, 19
Active voice, 42
Adjective clauses, 73
Adjectives, 46
    after direct objects, 52
    after linking verbs, 51
    compound, 47–48
    for comparisons, 53–58
    distinguished from adverbs, 49–51
    in series, 241–242
    irregular, 55
    nouns and pronouns as, 46–47
    placement of, 51–52
    prepositional phrases as, 60–61
    proper, 47–48
    special, 47–48
    use of, 46
Adverb clauses, 73–74
Adverbs, 48
    after direct objects, 52
    for comparisons, 53–58
    conjunctive, 62, 66–67, 240
    distinguished from adjectives, 49–51
    irregular, 55
    placement of, 51–52
    prepositional phrases as, 60
    sentence, 49
Agreement,
    of pronoun and antecedent, 102–104
    of sentence parts, 94–104

    of subject and verb, 95–102
Antecedents, 6, 17, 102–104
Appositive, 10–11, 240–241
Apostrophe, 257–260
Auxiliary verbs, 22
Brackets, 251–253
Capitalization, 263–265
Case,
    nominative, 9–11, 147
    objective, 9–13, 129, 147
    possessive, 15–17
Clauses, 72–75
    adjective, 73
    adverb, 73–74
    dependent, 72–75, 82–83, 87
    elliptical, 75
    independent or main, 72, 82–83,
        237–238, 243–244, 245
    non-restrictive, 240
    noun, 74–75
    restrictive, 239, 240
    subordinate, 72–75, 82–83, 87
Collective nouns, 5, 100–102, 111
Colon, 245–247
Comma, 237–243
Comma splice, 88
Common nouns, 4
Comparative degree, 53–56
Comparisons, incomplete, 56–57
Complements,
    object, 78–80
    sentence, 78–80
    subject, 21–22, 78, 80
Complex sentences, 82–83
    separating, 74

Compound,
    adjectives, 47–48
    nouns, 5
    sentences, 81–82
Compound-complex sentences, 83
Conditional, 39–40
Confused, words often, 167–199
Conjunctions, 61–68
    coordinating, 62–63
    correlative, 63–64
    and parallelism, 64
    subordinating, 64–66
Conjunctive adverbs, 62, 66–67, 238, 240
Coordinating conjunctions, 62–63
Copula, 20–22
Correlative conjunctions, 63–64
Dangling modifiers, 91–93
Dash, 247–249, 260
Degree,
    comparative, 53–56
    of adjectives and adverbs, 53–55
    positive, 53–55
    superlative, 54–56
Demonstrative pronouns, 8, 47
Dependent clauses, 72–75, 82–83, 87
Determiners, 45–46
Direct objects, 11–12, 78–79
Ellipsis, 249–250
Elliptical clauses, 75
Ergatives, 20
Errors, sentence, 86–94
Exclamation point, 237
Exclamatory sentences, 85
Forward slash, 257
Fragments, 86–88

Fused sentence, 88–89
Gender-neutral language, 201–206
Gerunds, 16, 44–45, 71
Helping verbs, 22
Hyphen, 260–263
Imperative mood, 40–41
Indefinite pronouns, 8–9, 47
Independent clauses, 72, 82–83, 237–238
Indicative mood, 40–41
Indirect object, 79
Infinitives, 24–25
Insensitive language, avoiding, 200–211
Intensive pronouns, 7, 151
Interjections, 68–69
Interrogative pronouns, 7, 47
Intransitive verbs, 19–20, 78
Irregular verbs, 26–30
Italics, 255–256
Linking verbs, 11, 20–22, 51, 80
Lists, parallel, 119
Misplaced modifiers, 90–91
Modal auxiliaries, 22–23
Modifiers,
    dangling, 91–93
    misplaced, 90–91
    squinting, 93–94
Mood,
    imperative, 41
    indicative, 40–41
    shifts in, 107–108
    of verbs, 40–42
    subjunctive, 41–42
Nominative case, 9–11, 147
Nonrestrictive phrases and clauses,
    puncuation with, 240

Noun clauses, 74
Nouns, 4–5
    as adjectives, 46–47
    case, 9–10
    collective, 5, 100–102, 111
    common, 4
    compound, 5
    mass, 5
    predicate monimative, 11, 80
    proper, 5
Number, shifts in, 110–112
Objective case, 9–13, 129, 147
Object complements, 79–80
Objects,
    direct, 78–79
    indirect, 79
    of preposition, 12, 59, 129
Offensive language, avoiding, 200–211
Outlines, parallel, 119
Parallel structure, 116–118
Parentheses, 250–251
Participles,
    past, 25–26
    present, 26
Parts of speech, 3–69
    see also specific parts of speech,
        e.g., Noun
Passive voice, 43–44
Period, 235–236
Person,
    of pronouns, 6–7
    shifts in, 108–110
Perspective, shifts in, 110
Phrasal,
    prepositions, 59

Phrasal (continued)
   verbs, 23
Phrases, 70–72
   noun, 70
   prepositional, 59–60, 70–71
   transitional, 67–68, 238
   verb, 70
   verbal, 71–72
Positive degree, 53–55
Possessive case, 9, 15–17
Predicate, 11, 76–77
Predicate nominative, 11, 80
Prefixes, 269–275
Prepositional phrases, 59–61, 70–71
Prepositions, 58–61
   and adverbs, 61
   phrasal, 59
   placement of, 60
   subordinating conjunctions versus,
      65–66
Progressive, 26, 35–38
Pronouns, 6–18
   as adjectives, 46–47
   agreement of sentence parts,
      94–95, 102–104
   ambiguous references, 17–18
   case, 9–17
   demonstrative, 8, 47
   indefinite, 8–9, 47
   intensive, 7, 151
   interrogative, 7, 47
   personal, 6–7
   predicate nominative, 11, 80
   relative, 8
   reflexive, 7, 151

Proper,
    adjectives, 47–48
    nouns, 5
Punctuation, 233–265
    see also specific types, e.g., Comma
Question mark, 236
Quotation marks, 253–255
Quotations,
    omissions: *see* Ellipsis
    shifts in, 114–115
Reflexive pronouns, 7, 151
Regular verbs, 26–27
Relative pronouns, 8
Restrictive phrases and clauses,
       punctuation with, 239–240
Roots, 287–301
Run-ons, 88–90
Semicolon, 243–245
Sentence errors, 86–94
Sentences,
    agreement of parts, 94–104
    complements, 78–80
    complex, 82–83
    compound, 81–82
    compound-complex, 83
    declarative, 84
    errors, 86–94
    exclamatory, 85
    formation of, 80–84
    fragments, 86–88
    function, 84–85
    imperative, 85
    interrogative, 84–85
    inverted, 78
    modifiers, 90–94

Sentences (continued)
objects, 78–80
parts of, 76–80
punctuation, 235–265
run-on, 88–90
simple, 81
Series,
comma in, 241–242
parallel structure in, 118–119
Sexist language, avoiding, 201–206
Shifts,
in mood, 107–108
in number, 110–112
in person, 108–110
in perspective, 110
in quotations, 114–115
in tense, 105–106
in tone and style, 112–114
in voice, 106–107
Slash, 257
Solidus, 257
Speech, parts of, 3–69
see also specific parts of speech, e.g.
Nouns
Spell checker, 231
Spelling,
rules of, 215–217
words often misspelled, 218–230
Squinting modifiers, 93–94
Style, shifts in, 112–114
Subject complements, 78, 80
Subordinate clauses, 72–75, 82–83, 87
Subordinating conjunctions, 64–66
Subjects,
agreement of sentence parts, 95–102

    complement, 80
    hard-to-locate, 76–78
    singular or plural, 94–104
Subjunctive mood, 41–42
Suffixes, 276–286
Superlative degree, 53–56
Tense,
    future, 33
    future perfect, 35
    past, 32–33
    past perfect, 34–35
    present, 31–32
    present perfect, 34
    sequence of, 38–40
    shifts in, 105–106
    simple, 30–33
    use of, 38–40
Tone, shifts in, 112–114
Transtional phrases, 67–68, 238
Transitive verbs, 19, 42, 78
Underlining, 255–256
Usage, 121–211
Verbals, 44–45, 71–72
Verbs, 19–45
    auxiliary, 22
    copula, 20–22
    ergative, 20
    forms, 24–30
    infinitives, 24–25
    intransitive, 19–20, 78
    irregular, 26–30
    linking, 11, 20–22, 51, 80
    modal, 22
    mood, 40–42
    participles, 25–26

Verbs (continued)
    phrasal, 23
    regular, 26–27
    tense of, 30–40
    transitive, 19, 78
    voice, 42–44
Virgule, 257
Voice,
    shifts in, 106–107
    of verbs, 42–44
Who and whom, uses of, 13–15
Word division, rules of, 232
Words often confused, 167–199